READING

COMPREHENSION FOR

2ND GRADE

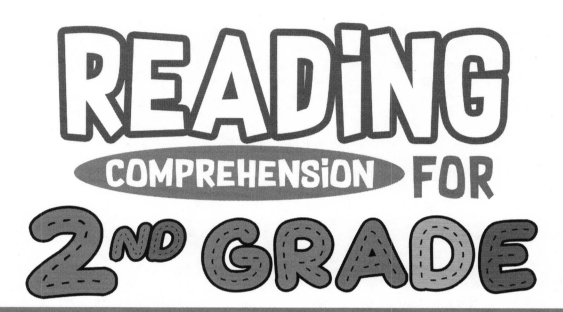

HIGHLY CONVENIENT - IDEAL FOR KIDS & SKILL ENHANCING 2ND GRADE READING BOOKS

Patrick N. Peerson

FUNNY learn PLAY

Reading Comprehension Grade 2
Highly Convenient

Ideal for Kids & Skill Enhancing
2nd Grade Reading Books

Transforming the learning capacity & capabilities of your kids ever so elegantly, our premium & wonderfully crafted 2nd grade reading books prove to be a vital addition in the learning books. Reading Comprehension Grade 2 book comes with modernly organized content which enables the kid to take their learning ability to a greater level grammar workbook grade 2

Features :

Reading comprehension grade 2 feature plenty of gradually advancing levels targets for the students and kids which is their essential requirement at a growing age for steady growth.

Books for 2nd graders comes with skill oriented stuff which is designed in such a way that the book enhances the skill level with ease by providing normal progression.

Spelling workbook grade 2 have more than 40 workbook pages which are filled with ready to reproduce pages so that the kids are offered with the wide variety for having to practice.

Workbooks for 2nd graders has too very easy to follow instructions and directions along with the entertaining exercises to motivate them to work on their own.

Spelling Wrkbook Grade 2 is drafted right according to relevant applied standards and ensures that a pragmatic approach for the betterment of students can be inculcated.

Patrick N. Peerson
Funny Learn Play

I'm A Monster!

Sarah put on a mask.

She looked in the mirror and laughed at her funny clothes. This is a great outfit. Sarah ran from her bedroom into her mom and dad's room.

"ROAR! I'm coming to eat you!" she shouted.
"Wonderful costume," said mom.
"Yes, I'm a monster," Sarah replied.

1. What was Sarah's outfit?
   a. A witch
   b. A monster
   c. An animal
   d. A fairy

2. Where did Sarah run to?
   a. Her brother's room
   b. The living room
   c. Her mom and dad's room
   d. The kitchen

3. Who saw Sarah?

_____

4. What did Sarah reply to her mom?

_____

Name:_____

First Boat Ride

Angie and her mom are going on a boat trip.
Angie's mom drives to the port.

   "This is my first time on a boat!"
Angie tells the crew member and the captain.

"Welcome aboard," says the captain.
"Have a great trip," says the crew member.

Angie and her mom sit down and look out of the window. The boat starts to move. Angie and her mom go for a walk on the boat's deck. Angie can feel the wind on her face as the boat sails across the water. They can see houses and shops next to the water. People wave as the boat passes. They see fish in the water.

   "I think I love boat rides; they are fun!" Angie says to mom.

1. Who drives to the port?_____

2. Who says "Welcome aboard," to Angie?
   a. The captain   b. Angie's mom
   c. Angie's dad   d. The waiter

3. What can Angie and her mom see in the water?

   _____

4. What does Angie think of this boat's ride?
       a. Great   b. Boring   c. Slow   d. Fun

The New Pencil Case

Carl's pencil case had scratches on it. It had a small dent too.
He wanted a nice new pencil case. Carl asked dad,
  "Please can I have a new pencil case?"
  "I'm sorry, son, but your old pencil case is still good for now,"
  dad said. Carl was sad. He thought for a few minutes.
  "Perhaps I can buy my own new pencil case.
  How much will it cost?"
  "Around three dollars," dad replied.

Carl went to the playroom and got his money box. He carefully counted all of his coins, but he had only one dollar.
  "I need to make more money!" thought Carl.

Carl thought and thought of different ways to get his new pencil case but he had no ideas. A few days later at school, Carl came top in his math test. His teacher gave him a sticker of a dinosaur. Carl stuck the sticker on his pencil case.

Carl did well in his schoolwork all week and got lots of stickers at school. He put them all on his pencil case. He then realized that he could use his one dollar to buy more stickers. He bought more stickers from the shop and completely covered his old pencil case. It looked like a new pencil case. All of the scratches were covered. Carl was happy with his pencil case.

1. How much would a new pencil case cost?

   _____

2. Which subject of school test did Carl come top in?

   _____

3. What was the first sticker Carl put on his pencil case?
   a. Dinosaur   b. Dragon   c. Bird   d. Dog

4. Which room did Carl keep his money-box?

   _____

Garden

Jordan and Lee were sitting in the garden. They were looking around at all plants, nature, and insects. They could see many interesting things.

Jordan saw a pretty flower.
   "Look at that beautiful pink flower," Jordan said.
   "That is not a flower," Lee said. "It's food for butterflies."

A butterfly came and landed on the flower and sipped the sweet nectar. Then, Jordan saw a small brown twig.
   "Look at that twig," said Jordan.
   "That is not a twig," Lee replied.
   "It's a building block for a bird's house."

Birds swooped down and picked up the little twig. They flew up on the tree and build their nest. Jordan saw a leaf.
   "Look at that green leaf," Jordan said.
   "That is not a leaf. It's a shady umbrella for beetles," Lee said.

A beetle crawled under the large leaf to escape from the sunshine. The garden is full of many useful things for nature!

1. Who are the two boys in the story?

_____

2. What was the second thing Jordan saw?

_____

3. What did Lee say about leaf?

_____

4. What color was the flower? _____

Sounds

He listened. These sounds were what he heard:
Children laughed as they played outside. His brother played soft music on the piano in the dining room. A door creaked.

A telephone rang shrilly somewhere in the house. The kettle bubbled and hissed as it boiled. His watch was ticking.

A van rumbled down the street. The washing machine whirred. Outside, a bird shrieked loudly. His cat purred in contentment.

The wind howled and whooshed. Somebody was using a lawnmower to cut their grass. The pages of his book quietly rustled as he turned a new page to read more.

1. **Which room was the piano in?**

   _____

2. **Fill in the blanks:**

   A _____ rumbled down the street.
   The washing machine _____.
   _____, a bird shirked _____.
   His cat _____ in contentment.
   The wind howled and _____.

3. **What was the creaking sound from?** _____

4. **Where did the children play?**

   _____

The Storm

The duck waddled quickly to the field, happy to have a picnic with her farmyard friends. She stopped and looked up. Big gray clouds filled the sky. She thought a storm was coming. Frightened, Duck started to hurry back to the barn.

She passed Chicken, Goat, and Sheep. "Why aren't you going to the field for our picnic?" Chicken asked. "I think the rain is coming. We should stay safe inside," Duck replied. Sheep looked at the clouds in the sky. "I think it will be fine. It doesn't look too bad," Sheep said. Duck still wasn't sure. "Up to you," Goat said. "We are still going to have fun at the picnic." The three friends left.

As Duck got closer to the barn, she also passed Pig, Horse, and Cow. All animals were excited about the picnic. The duck was happy to reach the shelter of the barn. She was worried about her friends, though.

Suddenly, thunder crashed in the air. Lightning bolts lit up the sky. The barn shook. Big drops of rain started to fall from the storm clouds. Duck looked outside. Her friends were running back to the barn. The ground outside was quickly muddy. The wind howled.

As the other farm animals charged into the barn, they moaned. "You were right!" Horse said. "We are so cold and wet!" Duck smiled. She was happy her friends were safe. They could have a picnic

1. What were three animals the duck see first?

_____

2. Which place did their friends plan to have a picnic?

a. at the farm   b. in the barn   c. in the forest   d. in the field

3. What crashed in the air? _____

4. Why did Duck smile?

_____

Wake Up

"I'm so sleepy today," said Rooster.
"I don't know if I will wake up on time in the morning."

"Don't worry," Cow said. "I'll moo very loudly to wake you."
"Who will wake you?" Rooster asked, worried.

"I'll wake Cow," Sheep said.
"I'll do my biggest baaaaa."

"But, who will wake you?"

"I'll wake Sheep," Pig said. "I'll grunt and oink like she's never heard before. But, someone must wake me first!"

"I'll wake Pig. I'll howl and bark until his eyes fly open," said Dog. "How will you wake up?" asked Sheep.

"No problem," said Dog.
"I always wake up as soon as I hear Rooster shout."

"What a good plan!" said Rooster as he started to laugh.

1. **How does Rooster feel at the start of the story?**

   _____

2. **Who will wake Sheep?**

   _____

3. **How will Dog wake Pig?**

   _____

4. **Fill in the gaps:**

   "What a _____ plan!" said _____ as he
   started to _____ .

The Missing Gloves

Grandma looked at the coat rack with a frown.

"My gloves aren't here," she said.

"Okay, Grandma, what are your gloves like?" Margie asked.

"They thick and brown," Grandma replied.

"When did you last wear them?" Brett asked.

"I wore them when I walked to the shop this morning. Then, I came back and hung them on the coat rack with my coat and scarf. They should be here, but they're not." Grandma said.

"Here are some gloves," Margie said. "But they are blue."

"No, they are Grandpa's gloves," Grandma said, still frowning.

"Here are some red gloves," Brett said.

"They are mine," said Margie.

"We need to look for brown gloves."

They looked in Grandma's coat pocket. There were no gloves. They looked on the floor. They looked behind the sofa. They looked in the kitchen. They could not find any brown gloves. Right then, Grandpa came through the door.

"Hi Grandpa, where did you go?" asked Brett.

"I took the dog for a walk in the park," Grandpa said.

"It's cold outside today!"

Margie started to giggle. "I know where your gloves are, Grandma. Look at Grandpa's hands." Grandpa was wearing thick, brown gloves.

"My gloves!" shouted Grandma. "Sorry. I didn't think you needed them, and they are warmer than mine," Grandpa said sheepishly.

"It's okay," said Grandma. "Now I can go and visit our neighbor with warm hands. Thank you for helping me look for my gloves, children."

1. **What was the color of Margie's gloves?** _____

2. **Where did Grandpa go?**
   a. To the shop   **b.** To a restaurant
   c. To visit a friend   **d.** To the park

3. **Who helped Grandma look for her gloves?**

   _____

4. **Who had Grandma's gloves?** _____

Clouds

Charlotte and her cousin, Jim,
were sitting outside in the garden.

There were many white,
fluffy clouds in the blue sky.

"Look," Charlotte pointed to the sky,
"What do you think that cloud looks like?"
"It looks like a clown," said Jim. "A clown cloud!"
"To me, it looks like a dragon," Charlotte said. "How about
    that one?" Charlotte pointed to a different cloud.
"I think it looks like an elf," said Jim.
"Hmmm. To me, it looks like a fairy," said Charlotte.

The two cousins continued looking at the shapes of the clouds.
"Oh no," said Charlotte as she pointed to a big gray cloud.
"What about that one?" Jim replied, "It looks like a duck."
"To me, it looks like rain!" Charlotte laughed.
A fat raindrop fell from the sky and plopped on the ground.
Then they ran back into the house.

1. **What is the relationship between Charlotte
   and Jim?** _____

2. **What does Charlotte think the first cloud
   looks like?** _____

3. **What does Jim think the gray cloud looks like?**

   _____

4. **Why did Charlotte and Jim run into the house?**

   _____

Bedtime Story

Willow loved listening to stories at bedtime. Willow's mom reads her a bedtime story every night. Sometimes the stories were about magical lands. Sometimes, they were about children. Some stories were about animals. Sometimes, she told stories about the holidays. Mom's bedtime stories are always fun!

Willow was excited about mom's newest story. But today, when bedtime comes, Dad takes Willow up to bed instead. He tucks her into bed and kisses her head.

"What about my story?" Willow asked.

"Tonight Mom is busy," Dad said. "Your little sister is sick.

But I can read you a bedtime story."

Dad tells a wonderful story about fairies and elves, unicorns, and animals. Willow falls asleep happy, thinking of a fairytale land.

1. Who always told Willow a bedtime story?

_____

2. Who is sick? _____

3. What does Dad tell Willow about story?
   (Complete the blank spaces)

   Fairies and _____ unicorns, and _____ .

4. What is Willow thinking about when she falls asleep?

   a. Her mom and dad   **b.** A fairytale land

   c. Dragons   **d.** School work

Name:_____

New Dress

Melanie loved her new dress.
It was a cool summer dress.
It was her favorite color pink.
It had lots of small flowers on it too.
And, best of all, it had two cute pockets.

It had hung in her closet for several weeks. She had waited for the spring getting warmer and the blooming flowers.

Then, the sun was shining, and birds sang on the green trees. Butterflies flitted between the flowers. It was a warm day.

Melanie could wear her new dress! She put on her new dress and went to play in the park with her friends.

1. **What was Melanie's new item of clothing?**
   a. Dress
   b. Shoes
   c. Skirt
   d. Coat

2. **What is Melanie's favorite color?**

   _____

3. **What were birds doing on the trees?**
   a. Singing
   b. Eating
   c. Sleeping
   d. Flying

4. **Where did Melanie go?**

   _____

Sunshine

One hot, sunny day, Dad picked up Danielle from school. When they arrived home, they went inside. It was cool because Dad put the air conditioning on.

"Today, it is too hot. I'm tired of the sun. I can't wait for the cooler winter," said Dad.

He sat down in the cool living room with a cold glass of water.

"I love the sunshine!" Danielle smiled. "I think I'll go and play with my friends for some time."

Danielle changed her clothes and ran outside. She met her friend's, Michelle and Debbie. They had fun outside in the sun.

They played jump rope. They threw the ball. They splashed water from the fountain. They sat in the shade of a tree and talked about pop music. Then, they all started to feel hot.

Danielle went home. She walked into the house, hot and sweaty. The air conditioning made her felt great!

"Here, drink this," Mom said. She gave Danielle a glass of chilled lemonade.

"Mmmm, I like lemonade," said Danielle as she took a big gulp and smiled.

1. Who picked up Danielle from school?

_____

2. What did dad drink?

_____

3. What did Danielle drink?

_____

4. What were Danielle's friends' names?

_____

Name: _____

Thai Islands

It was Carl's first time on the Thai Islands. His family had taken a vacation to a big island called Koh Samui. They were so many things to enjoy. Carl was amazed.

"Let's swim in the sea!" Carl shouted to his brother.
They ran into the soft waves, that the water was clear and cold.
"Now let's hunt for seashells," Carl said.
They walked along the sand, picking up colorful shells.

"Let's play Frisbee!" Carl said.
They threw the Frisbee back and forward to each other and ran on the soft, white sand.

"Now let's build a sandcastle," Carl said.
They dug a moat and collected buckets of sand to make a big, grand castle on the beach. Carl and his brother had a great day at the beach on the Thai Islands.

1. Which Thai Island did Carl visit? _____

2. What did Carl and his brother play with?
   a. A ball   b. An inflatable toy
   c. A kite   d. A Frisbee

3. What did the two brothers make on the beach?

   _____

4. What color is the sand on the island?

   _____

Spider Web

Mary was playing in the garden with her sister, Florence. She ran through a big spider's web by accident.

The sticky web stuck to her face and hair. She hopped and jumped, yelling. She quickly wiped her face and hair. Mary was scared of spiders!

"A spider! A spider's web! Where is it? Get the spider off me!" Mary rubbed her face and hair some more. She felt the sticky web on her fingertips.

"I can feel it! It's huge! The spider is on me," Mary screamed in horror.
"Can you find the spider?" She asked Florence.

Florence laughed. "I think that's the spider," Florence said as she pointed to the tree trunk. A small spider ran up the trunk and onto a leaf.

1. What is Mary's sister called?

_____

2. How did the web feel?
   a. Slimy   b. Sloppy
   c. Sticky   d. Soft

3. What did the spider run onto?

_____

4. Why was Mary upset?

_____

Carrot Cake

Wanda's school is having a cake sale.

What should Wanda take?
Chocolate brownies?
Lemon muffins?

Wanda looks in the kitchen cupboards. She thinks long and hard. She asks Mom for ideas.

"Mom, we have a cake sale at school. What can I make?"
Mom thinks too. "Shall we make a carrot cake?"
"That's a fantastic idea!" Wanda says happily.

Wanda and Mom bake a delicious carrot cake. All of Wanda's classmates love the tasty cake.

1. Who helps Wanda to making a cake?

   _____

2. What kind of cake that Wanda make?

   _____

3. Why does Wanda want to make a cake?
   a. For a cake sale at school
   b. For her friend's birthday
   c. For a party at Girl Scouts
   d. For a bake sale at her club

4. What does Wanda think of making before Mom had an idea? (Complete the spaces)

   _____ brownies or _____ muffins.

The Fox

One afternoon I saw something in the bushes. It was a small fox. It ran right past me. I wanted to see where it was going, so I chased after it.

The fox ran quickly. It was difficult to see. I ran faster. It ran behind a tree, through a bush. I could not find it.

Suddenly, I saw it again. It moved quickly. It was the fox! It ran into a hole. I ran towards the hole then hid behind a bush. I watched the fox come out of the hole with her baby foxes. They ate and played.

1. What kind of animal was in the story?

_____

2. What did the fox run through?

_____

3. What did the fox run into?

_____

4. What did the fox and her baby foxes do?

_____

Name:_____

Akash and Sarah

Akash and Sarah were playing on the beach.
They ran across the soft sand and paddled in the sea.
   "Let's collect some seashells," Sarah said to Akash.
   "Okay, I'd love to," Akash said.
They walked up and down the beach, picking up a beautiful collection of shells.
   "I know," Sarah said. "Let's build a big sandcastle and cover it with our shells."
   "What a great idea," Akash said.
So they collected buckets of sand, dug a hole for the moat, and filled it with water. When their sandcastle was finished, they carefully decorated it with their shells. Akash picked up a stick.
   "I'm going to draw a heart around our castle."
   "What a lovely idea," Sarah said.
They both smiled at their castle covered with shells and a big, beautiful heart.

1. What are the names of the two friends?

_____

2. Where were they playing?

_____

3. What did they build?

_____

4. What did Akash draw with a stick?
   a. Butterfly   **b.** Castle
   c. Flower   **d.** Heart

Sock Puppets

Ella, her sister Marie, and Grandma sat on the sofa.

"What shall we do tonight?" Ella asked.

"I know! Let's have a puppet show!" Marie said excitedly.

"But how?" asked Ella. "We haven't got any puppets."

"We can make them!" Marie said as she ran out of the room. She came back with the laundry basket and Grandma's sewing box.

"We can make faces on the socks!" Marie laughed.

So they each took a clean sock and sewed buttons for the eyes. They then stitched mouths on the socks with red cotton.

Marie put a sock over her hand, opened and closed her hand. The sock puppet looked like it was talking.

"Hello, I'm a baby sock," Marie giggled.

Ella laughed and grabbed her sock.

"Hi, I'm daddy sock."

They all laughed. Grandma made a deep voice and said, "Hello baby and daddy sock. I'm Grandpa sock."

Everyone laughed as they created their own sock puppet play. It was a fun evening.

1. Who suggested having a puppet show? _____

2. What did they use for eyes? _____

3. Complete the blank spaces:
   Grandma made a _____ voice and said,
   " _____ baby and _____ sock.
   I'm _____ sock."

4. What did Marie call her sock puppet?
   a. Mommy sock   b. Baby sock
   c. Grandma sock   d. Sister sock

The Funfair

At the weekend, Martha went to the funfair with her mom and dad. There were so many things to do! There were stalls selling cotton candy and ice cream, a small petting zoo, rides, and games. Martha raced around in the bumper cars and rode a fast roller coaster. She felt as though she was going into the clouds!

After the rides, Martha came to a games stand. She wanted to throw the small balls to knock over tin cans. The stall owner told her if she could knock down five cans she would win a prize. Martha looked at the prizes—there was a giant, colorful unicorn. She dearly wanted it. Martha aimed and threw with all of her power.

One can fell. Only four more!

Martha threw the rest of the balls and won her prize. She hugged her new unicorn all the way home.

1. **Where did Martha go with her mom and dad?**

   a. The park   **b.** The zoo

   c. The funfair   **d.** The supermarket

2. **What rides did Martha go on?**

   _____

3. **How many cans did Martha need to knock down to win a prize?** _____

4. **What did Martha get for a prize?**

   _____

Name:_____

Pepper Seeds

Barbara's mom gave her two pepper plant seeds.

"I want to see them grow," Barbara said.

"Seeds need water and sunlight to grow," her mom said. They planted the seeds in a jar, watered them, and placed them on the window ledge. The sunlight came through the window and warmed the jar. In a few days, the seeds had started to sprout. Barbara was excited.

"Look, mom! My pepper seeds are growing!"

"If you take good care of them, they will continue to grow," mom said. "Make sure they have enough water and don't move them from the sunlight." The seedlings continued to grow. Barbara was happy.

"I helped the seeds to grow. I gave them everything they needed."

1. How many pepper seeds did Barbara have?

_____

2. What two things do seeds need to grow?

_____

3. Where did Barbara put her jar on?

_____

4. Complete the blank spaces:
   Barbara was _____ . "I helped the_____
   to grow. I _____ them _____ they
   needed."

Pets

Many people have pets. Some people have dogs as pets. Others have cats. Some people have fish, turtles or rabbits.

Grandpa is not like most people. His three pets are hamsters. They are all girls. One is called Kylie, one is called Kay and the other is called

1. How many pets does Grandpa have?

_____

2. What animals does Grandpa have?

_____

3. Is Kay a boy or a girl?

_____

4. Fill in the spaces:

Some people have _____ as pets. Others have _____ . Some people have _____ , turtles or rabbits.

The Ring

Joanne found a ring.
Whose ring is it?

Is it Shelley's ring?
No. Shelley's ring is silver.
This ring is gold.

Is it Debbie's ring?
No. Debbie's ring has a big pink stone.
This ring has a big blue stone.

Is it Sharon's ring?
No. Sharon's ring has small purple stones.
This ring has small yellow stones.

Joanne did not know what to do with the ring.
Just then, Paula walked into the classroom.
"Oh, my ring!" cried Paula. "I'm so happy you found it!"

Joanne was happy to find the ring's owner.
Paula was happy to have her ring back.

1. Who found a ring?

   _____

2. Whose ring has a big pink stone?

   _____

3. What was Paula happy about?

   _____

4. Where did Joanne and Paula see each other?

   _____

Name: _____

What is It?

Shona was sleepy. She went upstairs to her bedroom.
It was time for bed. She brushed her teeth, changed into
her pajamas, and climbed into bed.
She snuggled underneath her duvet.

Suddenly, she heard her door quietly creaking open.
It was dark and she couldn't see what made the sound.
She called to her sister,
   "Sophie! Is that you?" There was no reply.
She shouted to her brother,
   "Toby, are you there?"
Again, there was no reply. Then, something jumped onto her
bed. It jumped across her and licked her face.
Shona giggled. It was Fluff, her playful puppy.

1. What did Shona brush?
   a. Her hair   **b.** Her puppy
   c. Her clothes   **d.** Her teeth

2. What sound did the door make?
   a. Squeak   **b.** Creak
   c. Groan   **d.** Bang

3. What is Shona's brother called?

_____

4. What jumped on Shona's bed?

_____

My White Dog

I have a pet dog.
She is big and white.
She is called Marley.

We play with a stick. I throw a stick for Marley.
She runs after it and brings it back to me.

I throw the stick again.
It goes into the pond.
Marley splashes in the water to fetch the stick.
She brings it back.

1. What color is Marley?

_____

2. What does Marley play with?

_____

3. Where does the stick go?

_____

4. What does Marley do with the pond?

_____

Name: _____

My Playful Kitten

My kitten is very playful. She loves to play with everything. She plays with toy mice, balls, bells and string.

My kitten found a ball of yarn. It was white. My kitten pulled and chased the yarn.

My kitten found a ball. It was red. She rolled the ball underneath the sofa.

My kitten found a toy mouse. It was blue. She chewed the toy mouse.

My kitten found a bell. It was yellow. She made lots of noise with the bell. My kitten is now very tired!

1. What color was the toy mouse?

_____

2. What did the kitten pull and chase?

_____

3. What was red?

_____

4. What did the kitten make lots of noise with?

_____

Barbecue

Lenny walked into the back garden with his dad. He helped his dad pile coals on the grill and watched his dad start the fire. The coals began to smoke.

Mom carried out a tray of meat. Dad put the food on the barbecue. The smell was delicious! Lenny sniffed and inhaled the tempting smells. "Yum!"

Their pet dog ran over, wagging his tail. "Woof!"
"I think someone else is excited for BBQ, too!" laughed Lenny.
"It won't be long," dad said. "Help mom bring the salad and bread to the table."

Lenny and the dog ran into the kitchen. The dog picked up his ball and looked at Lenny. Lenny played with his dog.
He forgot what his dad asked him to do.

"BBQ time!" shouted dad.
Lenny ran to the garden. There was no salad. There was no bread. He quickly ran back to the kitchen to help mom.
He was excited to eat the delicious grilled meats.

1. Who started the fire? _____

2. What two things did Lenny need to take to the table for mom? _____

3. Fill in the black spaces:
   Lenny and the _____ ran into the _____.
   The dog picked up his _____ and looked at Lenny. Lenny _____ with his dog.
   He _____ what his dad asked him to do.

4. What was Lenny excited to eat?_____

Harvest Time

Sophie and Grandpa planted seeds in the garden. They wanted to grow their own fresh vegetables.

Sophie and Grandpa waited for the plants to grow. When the time passed, they watered the seedlings and made sure the birds couldn't eat them.

"When can we pick the radishes?" Sophie asked.
"Tomorrow," replied Grandpa.
"When can we pick the carrots?" Sophie asked.
"Tomorrow," replied Grandpa.
"When can we pick the peas?" Sophie asked.
"Tomorrow," replied Grandpa.

Sophie waited for the sun to shine down on her garden the next day. She wore her old clothes and put on her gardening gloves.

"Grandpa! It's time!" Sophie called out in excitement. Together, Sophie and Grandpa harvested their vegetables. They picked radishes, carrots, and peas. They were both happy with their garden.

1. Who did Sophie plant seeds with?_____

2. What seeds did Sophie plant?

_____

3. When did Grandpa say they could harvest the vegetables?
   a. Today   b. Saturday
   c. Thursday   d. Tomorrow

4. How did Sophie and Grandpa feel at the end of the story?_____

Lunch Time

Rana's mom is making lunch. She is making vegetable pasta, garlic bread, and salad. Rana and her sister, Betty, want to help.

Rana put cucumber in the salad.
She spread garlic butter on the bread.

Betty washed lettuce leaves for the salad. She set the table. When lunch was ready, they called their brother and dad.

"Martin! Dad! Lunch is ready!"

Martin and dad washed their hands and sat at the table. The family enjoyed a delicious lunch together.

When everyone finished eating Dad, and Martin washed the dishes. Rana, Betty, and Mom sat in the garden

1. **Which meal was Mom making?**

   _____

2. **What did Rana put in the salad?**
   a. Cucumber
   b. Carrot
   c. Lettuce
   d. Tomato

3. **Who set the table?**

   _____

4. **Who washed the dishes?**

   _____

A Cold Day in Winter

We get ready for school. It's cold outside, so we dress warmly.
We wear our winter coats, scarves, gloves, and hats over our
school uniform.

We drink hot chocolate before we leave the house.
The wind blows coldly around us as we wait for the school bus.
We can see our breath in the icy air.

The blue bus drives towards us.
"Get on, it's cold outside today!" the driver says.
We sit down on the bus. At outside, the trees have no leaves.
There's snow on the ground. The road is slippery.

The bus is nice and warm. We arrive at school.
We shiver as we get off the bus. The path is slippery.
We walk as fast as we can to our warm classroom.

We take off our coats, scarves, gloves, and hats.
We blow on our hands to warm them up.
Our classroom is nice and warm. Our teacher is happy.

1. **What is the weather like outside?** _____

2. **What color is the school bus?** _____

3. **How do the bus and classroom feel?**

   _____

4. **Fill in the blank spaces:**
   We arrive at _____ . We shiver as we get off
   the _____ . The path is _____ . We walk
   as fast as we can to our warm _____ .
   We take off our _____ , scarves, _____ ,
   and hats. We blow on our _____ to warm
   them up.

The Best

Tom and Tim are brothers. Tom is slow and careful.
Tim is quick and always wants to be the first.
He thinks that being first is the best.

"I can eat my dinner quicker. I am the best!" Tim said.

"I taste my food and eat slower. I don't care about
being first. I want to enjoy my meal." Tom said.

"I can finish my school work first. I am the best!" Tim said.

"I don't care about being first," Tom replied.

"I want to do my work well."

"I can run up the stairs quicker. I am the best!" Tim said.

"I don't want to fall down.

I am happy to be careful." Tom said.

Tim rushed to zip up his jacket. He hurried so much the zip got
stuck. He couldn't fasten up his jacket to go to school.

Tom looked."It would help if you slowed down," he said.
He carefully helped Tim to free the zip.

"Thank you, Tom," Tim said. "You're the best!"

1. Which brother wants to be the best?

_____

2. What can Tim run up quicker?

_____

3. What does Tom want to enjoy?

_____

4. What part of jacket does Tim have problems with?

_____

Twins

Lee and Lisa are brother and sister. They are twins. They look very alike. They have very different personalities, though. They are very different people.

Lee loves to eat sweet food, like cake and chocolate. Lisa prefers savory food, like pizza and chips.

Lee's favorite subject in school is art. Lisa's favorite subject is sport.

Lee likes comic books. Lisa likes storybooks.

Lee's favorite color is green. Lisa's favorite color is purple.

Lee is quiet and shy. Lisa is loud and talkative.

There are many differences between the twins. They look alike on the outside, but inside they are different. They are still best friends though, and love each other lots.

1. **What are the names of the twins?**

   _____

2. **What kind of books does Lee like?**

   _____

3. **Whose favorite color is purple?**

   _____

4. **Which twin is shy?**

   _____

Games

Charlie and Phoebe are playing games at home.
They decide to play hide and seek. Charlie closes his eyes
and counts 1 to 50. Phoebe runs to hide.
  "Ready or not, here I come!" Charlie shouts.
He looks in the living room. He looks behind the sofa.
He looks under the table. He looks behind the table, but
still cannot find Phoebe.

Charlie goes into the hall. He cannot see Phoebe.
He goes into the kitchen. He looks behind the door.
  "Found you!" He shouts. But it is a cat.
  "Found you!" He opens the cupboard quickly,
  but he only finds snacks.
Then, he hears a quiet giggle. He watches the cat walk to
the side of the washing machine. He follows the cat.
He finds Phoebe curled up in a small space between the
wall and the washing machine.
  "Found you!" He shouts.

1. **Which room does Charlie look for her first?**
   a. Living room   **b.** Dining room
   c. Kitchen   **d.** Bedroom

2. **What is Charlie's friend called?**

   _____

3. **What does Charlie find behind the kitchen door?**

   _____

4. **What is the word does Charlie shout?**

   _____

Play Time

"Can we play a game?" Lucy asked her brother Ben.
"Even though I'm bored, I need to do my math homework.
Maybe later." Ben replied.

"OK. I have an idea. I'm your teacher!" Lucy said.
"Open your math book." Ben opened his book.
"Sharpen your pencil," Lucy said. Ben sharpened his pencil.

"Now take your exercise book out of your bag. Open a new
page and write the date at the top. Draw a line under the
date." Ben did what Lucy told him to.

"Now, read the problems and write the answers in your
exercise book." Lucy watched as Ben completed his
homework.

When he had finished, Lucy said, "Now, close your books
and put them back in your bag." Ben smiled. "Thank you
Lucy. You helped me to do my homework." Lucy laughed.
"No, we played a game!"

1. Who wanted to play?_____

2. What homework did Ben do?_____

3. What did Ben write first at the top of the page?

_____

4. Where did Ben put his books when he finished
   his homework?

    a. On his desk   **b.** In his bag
    c. On a shelf   **d.** In his cupboard

Vampire Cat

After lunch, Mom said to Kayla,
  "Let's rearrange and tidy your bedroom."
  "Yes," said Kayla. "Oscar can help as well." Kayla said to her cat.
Kayla called her cat, but he didn't come.
  "Oscar! Oscar! Where are you?"
  "Do you know where Oscar is?" Kayla asked Mom.
  "I'm not sure. I did see him in my bedroom this morning, though." Mom replied.
  "I'll go and look for him," Kayla said.

She went into Mom's bedroom and called her cat.
  "Oscar! Come here boy." She couldn't see Oscar.

She pulled back the blanket on Mom's bed. Oscar was underneath, curled up. The sheet was draped over his head like a cloak. He looked like a vampire!
  "Oh, Oscar. There you are! You look just like a vampire. I think that's what you should be at a costume party!"

1. **What room did Kayla and Mom plan to rearrange and tidy?** _____

2. **What kind of animal is Oscar?**

   _____

3. **What room did Kayla find Oscar in?**

   _____

4. **What did Oscar look like?**
      a. Vampire   **b.** Turtle   **c.** Ghost   **d.** Postman

Collections

Charlotte and her brother Max are at the beach.

Charlotte likes to collect seashells. She thinks the seashells are beautiful. She walks along the beach, looking for pretty shells. Max follows her.

Charlotte picks up a shell.

"Oh, there's a crab under this shell," Charlotte shouts.

Charlotte picks up another shell.

"Oh, there's so much sand on this shell," Charlotte says.

Charlotte walks over to another shell.

"Oh, there's another crab!" she screams.

Charlotte continues to look for pretty seashells.

Max keeps following her.

"Max, why are you right behind me?

Why are you following me?"

Max laughed. He showed her inside his bucket.

"I'm collecting crabs!"

1. What is under the third shell that Charlotte picks up? _____

2. What is Charlotte's brother called?

_____

3. What is Max collecting?

_____

4. Where does this story take place?

_____

Lunch Time

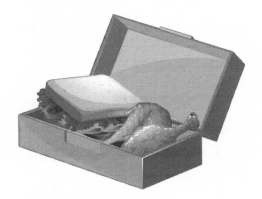

Marie and Anda sit down to eat lunch together.

"What's in your lunch box?" Marie asks Anda.
"I have a cheese sandwich today. I also have
orange juice and an apple." Anda replied.
"What's in your lunch box?" Anda asks Marie.
"I have a ham sandwich. I have a bottle of water
and yogurt as well." Marie replied.

They both enjoy their lunch together.

1. Who has an apple in the lunch box?

   _____

2. Who has a yogurt?

   _____

3. What kind of sandwich does Marie have?

   _____

4. Which meal are the two friends eating?

   _____

Making Pizza

"What are you doing?" Tony asked his big sister Joy.
"I'm making a pizza," Joy replied.
"Can I help?" asked Tony.
"Sorry, no. You're too small to make pizza," Joy told him.

Tony watched as Joy mixed flour, water, salt, and yeast together to make the pizza base.

He watched her chop vegetables to put on top of the pizza. She chopped onions, tomatoes, and peppers. She also had a jar of olives.

Joy spread tomato paste on the pizza base. She was about to sprinkle the toppings on top.
    "Wait a moment!" Tony shouted.
    He ran to the refrigerator. "You forgot the cheese!"
    "Ah, thank you," Joy said. I guess you're not too little to help after all!"

1. **Complete the blank spaces:**

    He watched her chop _____ to put on top of the _____. She chopped _____, tomatoes, and _____ . She also had a jar of olives.

2. **What is Joy mixing with flour, water, salt, and yeast for?** _____

3. **What did Joy forget?**

    _____

4. **What is the relation between Tony to Joy?**

    _____

Name: _____

Family Dinner

The Jones family was eating dinner together.

Around the table were Mom and Dad and their three children, Terry, Sandra, and Paul.

"Thanks, Mom. That was delicious!"

Sandra said when they finished eating.
   "Yes, thanks, Mom. What's for dessert?" Terry asked.
   "Chocolate brownie with ice cream. You can choose chocolate, vanilla, or strawberry ice cream," Mom replied.
   "Yum! I'll have chocolate ice cream, please!" Terry said.
   "Can I have strawberry, please?" Sandra asked.
   "And, all three flavors for me, please!" Paul laughed.

1. What are Sandra's two brothers called?

   _____

2. What is for dessert?

   _____

3. Who wants all three flavors of ice cream?

   _____

4. What flavor ice cream does Terry want?

   _____

The Pet Shop

Mom and Dad took Sally and James to the pet shop. There were many animals. There were puppies, kittens, rabbits, hamsters, mice, fish, birds, lizards, snakes, and more.

James wanted to get a mouse.
   "We are not getting a mouse, they scare me," Mom said.

Sally wanted to get a puppy.
   "We are not getting a puppy.
   They need too much time and money," Dad said.

They thought about getting a kitten or a hamster.
They knew they could only have one pet.

Eventually, Sally and James agreed to get a rabbit.
They are cute and friendly. They chose a small brown rabbit and called her Floppy.

1. Where did Mom and Dad take their two children?

_____

2. Why didn't Mom want a mouse?

_____

3. What color is the new pet?

_____

4. What kind of animal is Floppy?

_____

School work

Carol and Alice are doing their school homework together.

Carol loves math, and Alice loves art. Alice has ten math questions to do. Carol helps Alice with her math homework.

Then, Carol needs to draw something for her art homework. Alice shows her how to draw nicely.

They then do their English reading homework together.
   "That was a lot of homework!" said Alice.
   "Yes. Now we should play!" said Carol.
The two friends skip into the garden.

1. What school subject does Carol like?

_____

2. What homework does Alice help Carol with?

_____

3. Who suggests going to play?

_____

4. Where do the friends go to play?

_____

Name: _____

Andrew's New Pants

Andrew loved his old blue pants.
They were his favorite thing to wear!
His old blue pants felt soft.
His old blue pants had two pockets. Andrew
thought his old blue pants were just right!
One day his mom said that they were going to
the store. She said they were going to buy
some new pants for him.
"Why?" asked Andrew. "
I already have my old blue pants."
"You are getting taller, Andrew," said his mom.
"Your old blue pants are not big enough for you anymore."
Andrew did not like hearing this. He did not want new pants.
At the store, Andrew and his mom looked at all the colors of
pants. There were green pants, black pants, brown pants, gray
pants, and... blue pants! When Andrew tried on the new blue
pants, he realized they felt soft. He realized that they had two
pockets. He realized that they were just right!

1. Where did Andrew and his mom go?
   _____
2. How many pockets did Andrew's pants have?
   _____
3. How did Andrew's pants feel? _____
4. Why did Andrew need new pants?
   a. There were holes in his old pants.
   b. Andrew didn't like the color blue.
   c. Andrew was getting taller.
   d. The old pants had no pockets.

Danielle and the Dinosaurs

Danielle was spending the day with her family in the city. They were visiting a museum. When they arrived, they got a map of all the exhibits in the museum.

"What should we look at first?" asked her dad.

"Which way should we go?" asked her mom.

Danielle looked at the map. There were many exhibits, but Danielle knew where she wanted to go!

"Let's go to see the dinosaurs!" Danielle said excitedly.

"That is where I want to go too!" said Danielle's little sister.

They followed the map to the dinosaur exhibit.

"Wow! Look how big they are!" Danielle said. She was amazed at the giant dinosaur bones that were in the exhibit. Danielle liked the Triceratops dinosaur the best. Danielle and her family spent most of their visit looking at the dinosaurs. It was a wonderful day at the museum!

1. Where was the museum?_____

2. Which dinosaur was Danielle's favorite?
   a. Stegosaurus
   b. Tyrannosaurus Rex
   c. Brontosaurus
   d. Triceratops

3. What did the family use to help find their way to the dinosaur exhibit? _____

4. Does Danielle have a little brother or a little sister?

_____

Joey and the Lost Book

Joey loved to read books. He liked books about animals. He liked books about outer space. He liked books about sports. Reading books was his favorite activity.

Last week Joey borrowed three books from the library. He was very careful with these books. He never got them dirty and was careful not to rip the pages.

"We are going to the library today," said Joey's mom. "Please gather your three library books to return."

Joey went to gather his books. He kept them in his bedroom. Two books were on his shelf, but one book was missing! Joey felt worried. He had never lost a book before…where could it be?

Joey looked under his bed, but it was not there. Joey looked in the kitchen, but it was not there. Joey looked on the couch in the family room, but it was not there.

Joey had one more place to look.

He went to his sister's bedroom.

She was reading his book!

"I like to read books too!" said his sister.

Joey felt so happy that he finally found the book!

1. **What is Joey's favorite activity?**

   _____

2. **How many books did Joey get from the library?**

   _____

3. **In which room of the house is the couch?**
   - a. The kitchen
   - b. The bedroom
   - c. The family room
   - d. The bathroom
4. **Who was reading the lost book?** _____

Name:_____

Molly's Special Day

There was a big calendar hanging on the wall of the kitchen.
Molly looked at it and felt very excited. Only one more day to
wait. Tomorrow was Molly's special day!
Molly's mom was getting ready for the special day by baking a
cake. It was going to be a chocolate cake with chocolate
frosting and strawberries on top.
Molly's dad was getting ready for the special day by working on
a surprise present for Molly.
It was hidden in the garage under a big sheet.
Molly's sisters were getting ready for the special day by hanging
up decorations. They used colorful streamers and balloons to
make the house look so pretty.
"I can't wait for tomorrow!" exclaimed Molly.
"It is going to be my special day!"
Can you guess why tomorrow
is going to be special for Molly?
It is going to be her birthday!

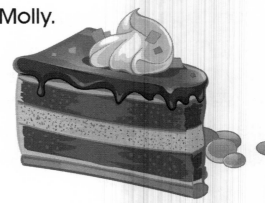

1. In which room of the house was the calendar?

_____

2. How did Molly's sisters make the house look pretty?
    a. They painted the walls a new color.
    b. They washed the floor.
    c. They hung up decorations.
    d. They planted flowers.

3. What kind of fruit was on the cake? _____

4. Where was Dad hiding Molly's present?

_____

Owen's New Neighbors

The house next door to Owen's house was empty.
Owen felt sad that he did not have any neighbors.
One morning Owen woke up to loud noises.
He didn't know where they were coming from.
Owen looked out his window and saw that
there was a big truck.
People were moving things from
the big truck into the empty house next door.
He saw a man moving a table.
He saw a woman moving a large box.
He saw a boy moving a suitcase.
"Mom! Dad!" Owen shouted. "Look what is happening outside!"
"Yes," said his mom, "we are getting new neighbors!"
"The new neighbors are a family with a mom,
a dad, and a boy the same age as you!" said his dad.
Owen became very excited.
He and his mom baked cookies to bring to the new neighbors.
Owen did not feel sad anymore!

1. Why did Owen feel sad?

   _____

2. How many people are in the new family next door?

   _____

3. What did Owen and his mom bake for his new neighbors?

   _____

4. What was the boy moving into the house?
      a. A table
      b. A teddy bear
      c. Some fruit
      d. A suitcase

The Big Surprise

The telephone rang at Gavin's house. It was his friend Charlie.

"Can you come to my house?" Charlie asked.

"Yes, I can come in the afternoon," said Gavin.

"Great," said Charlie, "I have a big surprise to show you!"

Gavin wondered what the surprise could be. Was the surprise a new toy? Was the surprise a new book? Was the surprise a cake? He was excited to see the surprise!

After Gavin ate his lunch, his mom drove him to Charlie's house. Charlie was waiting by the door with a big smile.

"Come inside to see the big surprise!" said Charlie.

Gavin walked into the house and saw Charlie's surprise! The surprise was a new puppy! The puppy had brown fur and a curly tail. Gavin thought the puppy was very cute!

"This puppy is a very big surprise!" said Gavin happily.

1. What was Charlie's surprise?
   a. a new book
   b. a puppy
   c. a cake
   d. a new toy

2. Who drove Gavin to Charlie's house?
   _____

3. What color was the puppy?
   _____

4. When did Gavin go to Charlie's house, in the afternoon or in the morning? _____

The Night Hike

Tristan was going camping with his dad. They were going camping in the woods.

During the daytime, Tristan and his dad did many fun activities. They went fishing, and they swam in the lake. They played some card games, and they went on a nature hike.

"I like to see trees and animals in the woods. I like to see all of nature!" Tristan said while they were on the hike.

His dad said, "Did you know there are some parts of nature we can only see at night?" Tristan was surprised. He thought that at night it would be too dark to see anything. That evening before they went to sleep in their tent, Tristan's dad said, "Let's go on a night hike!" On the night hike, Tristan saw animals that had been sleeping during the daytime. He saw the moon and many stars shining in the dark sky. Tristan loved seeing nature on their night hike!

1. With whom did Tristan go camping?
   _____

2. What did they do in the lake?
   a. washed the dishes
   b. rode in a boat
   c. went skiing
   d. went fishing and swimming

3. Name three things that Tristan saw on the night hike.
   _____

4. What kind of games did they play?
   _____

The Orchestra

Adrian was having a good day at school. It was Friday, and on Fridays his class always went to Mr. Smith's room to learn about music. Adrian thought that Mr. Smith was a fun music teacher!
"Have you ever heard an orchestra perform?" asked Mr. Smith. Most of the students in Adrian's class said they had never heard an orchestra perform. But not Adrian!
"Yes!" said Adrian. "I heard an orchestra perform!
I went to a concert in the city with my family."
Adrian told the class about going to the orchestra concert.
He told them about the violins, the violas, and the basses.
He told them about the trumpets, the tubas,
and the oboes. He told them about his favorite
instrument of all—the cello!
Mr. Smith felt very pleased that Adrian knew
so much about orchestras. Mr. Smith and
the class then listened to some orchestra music.
Adrian really enjoyed it!

1. What day of the week did Adrian's class
go to Mr. Smith's room? _____
2. Where did Adrian go to see the orchestra concert?

_____

3. What did the class listen to with Mr. Smith?

_____

4. Which orchestra instrument is Adrian's favorite?
    a. the cello
    b. the violin
    c. the tuba
    d. the viola

Name:_____

The Piano Lesson

Natalie's cousin Patrick knew how to play the piano.
She loved to hear him play.
Natalie dreamed of learning
how to play the piano too!

One day Natalie visited Patrick's house.
She admired his big piano with its
many black and white piano keys.

"Natalie, do you want to play the piano?" asked Patrick.
"Yes, I do!" Natalie exclaimed.
"Let's have a piano lesson!" said Patrick.
Patrick showed Natalie how to place her fingers on the piano keys.
He taught Natalie a simple song. Natalie felt very excited.
"Who is making such beautiful music?" asked her mom when she
walked into the room. "I am!" exclaimed Natalie.
"Patrick gave me a piano lesson!"
"Natalie is a wonderful piano student," said Patrick.
"Thank you, Patrick!" she said and gave her cousin a big hug.

1. **What does Natalie dream about?**

   _____

2. **Who is Natalie's cousin?**

   _____

3. **Where is the piano?**
      a. In the school
      b. In Patrick's house
      c. In a store
      d. In Grandma's house

4. **How does Natalie feel when playing the piano?**

   _____

The Rainy Day

Mia felt disappointed as she watched the drops of rain slide down the car window. She and her dad were going to visit her grandma and grandpa's house.

When Mia visited her grandma and grandpa, she liked to play in their big yard and look for sunny day treasures there. Mia liked to find pretty flowers growing in the grass. She liked to look for colorful rocks near the trees. She could not do these things in the rain.

Mia's grandpa was waiting by the door when they arrived.

"Come Mia! I want to show you something," said her grandpa. They looked at some old photographs in a big book. The photographs were of Mia's dad when he was younger. Mia liked seeing the old photographs.

"Come Mia! I want to show you something," said her grandma. They looked at a closet filled with old games and puzzles. They belonged to Mia's dad when he was younger.

Mia liked playing with them.

Mia felt happy. The inside of her grandma and grandpa's house was filled with rainy day treasures... photographs, games, puzzles, and, best of all, her grandma and grandpa!

1. Why was Mia feeling disappointed?

   _____

   _____

2. What did Mia's grandpa show her? _____

3. What was in the closet?
   a. Games and puzzles
   b. Hats and mittens
   c. Cookies and candy
   d. A new computer

4. How did Mia feel at the end of the story? _____

A Day at the Beach

Caroline woke up early. She felt excited about today. Her family was going to the beach! Her mom, her dad, her sister, and her brother were all going to the beach.

At the beach, Caroline liked to play in the sand with her sister. They used a little shovel and a pail to help them build a sandcastle. They imagined that a princess lived in the sandcastle!

Caroline and her brother went swimming in the water. Their dad went swimming too. The water felt so good after playing in the hot sun. Caroline had fun jumping in the waves!

"Time for lunch!" called Caroline's mom.

"Hooray!" shouted Caroline. She felt very hungry!

The family ate sandwiches and chips. They also ate some apples and cookies. The lunch tasted so good!

"A day at the beach is the best kind of day!" exclaimed Caroline.

1. Which people went swimming?

   _____

2. What kind of fruit did they eat?_____

3. What did Caroline and her sister use to build the sandcastle?
    a. a little shovel and a pail
    b. a big bag and a spoon
    c. a comb and a little shovel
    d. a bowl and a big spoon

4. Which meal of the day did the family eat at the beach?

   _____

Amy's Vacation

Amy and her family were going on a big vacation. They were going to Disney World! Disney World was very far from Amy's home. They were going to fly to Disney World by airplane.

Amy was nervous about flying in an airplane. She had never been in one before. She was not sure if she would like being so high up in the sky!

On the airplane, Amy was surprised to see so many seats! She sat in a seat between her mom and her dad.

"Now you need to put on your seatbelt," said her dad. He showed Amy how to put on the seatbelt.

Amy's mom held her hand. She knew that Amy felt a bit nervous. The airplane started to move. It went very fast! Soon they were up in the air!

"Look!" said her mom. Amy looked out the little window. She could see the world below. It looked so tiny! Amy was not nervous anymore. She was enjoying the airplane ride!

1. Where was Amy going on vacation? _____
2. How did Amy feel before going on the airplane?
   _____
3. What did Amy's dad show her how to do?
   _____
4. What did Amy see out the window?
   a. the airplane
   b. the birds
   c. the world below
   d. her mom

Colors in the Sky

One rainy day Marie was using her crayons to draw a picture. The picture was a present for her grandma. Marie was drawing a picture of pink, purple, and yellow flowers.

Marie's grandma was coming to her house to visit. When Marie was done drawing the picture, she waited for her grandma by the window. Marie felt happy that her grandma was coming!

"Grandma is here!" Marie exclaimed when she saw Grandma's big white car.

Marie ran to the door with the picture for her grandma.

"I have a colorful surprise for you, Grandma!" Marie said when she opened the door for her grandma.

"And I have a colorful surprise for you!" said her grandma. "Look!"

Marie's grandma pointed to the sky.

There was a beautiful rainbow!

Marie loved seeing all the colors in the sky!

1. What did Marie use to draw the picture?

_____

2. How did Marie's grandma get to Marie's house?
   a. by train
   b. by car
   c. by airplane
   d. by bus

3. Where was Marie waiting for her grandma?

_____

4. What colorful surprise did Marie's grandma show to Marie?

_____

Gregory's Trip to the Moon

Gregory looked at the night sky.
He liked to see the moon. He told his mother,
"I will go to the moon." She laughed and told him
it was time to go to sleep.
The next day, Gregory woke up and looked outside.
It was a very windy day. He looked at the sky and could
still see the moon a little bit.
Gregory went downstairs and grabbed his biggest kite. He ran
outside. He flew his kite. The wind pulled the kite very quickly,
and he went up with it!
He looked up and saw that he was moving very close to
the moon! A few minutes later, he landed on the moon
and started to look around.
He was very excited to be on the moon, but he soon became
lonely. Then he remembered something he had learned in school:
there was no wind on the moon! How would he ever get back?
Gregory woke up and realized it was a dream. He laughed. He was
very happy to be on Earth.

1. Who told Gregory to go to sleep?

   _____

2. Was the weather outside very windy or very snowy?

   _____

3. What did Gregory use to get to the moon?
   a. a plane
   b. a boat
   c. a kite
   d. a truck

4. Did Gregory really go to the moon?

   _____

Lisa's New School

Lisa felt nervous. Tomorrow was her first day at a new school. Her family had just moved to a new town, and she did not know any other children at the new school. She did not know her new teacher.

"Do not worry," said her mother. "You will make a new friend."

"Do not worry," said her father. "Your new teacher will be nice."

The next morning Lisa woke up early. She put on her favorite red sweater. Her mother walked with her to the new school.

"Hello! My name is Miss Hoover. I am your new teacher!" said a lady who was standing by the door. She showed Lisa to the classroom.

Lisa walked into the classroom. There were many children there.

One girl smiled at Lisa.

She was wearing a red sweater too!

"Hi! My name is Janine.

Do you want to sit by me?" said the girl.

Lisa smiled. She did not feel nervous anymore.

She had a new friend!

Lisa liked her new school!

1. Why was Lisa going to a new school?

_____

2. What color was Lisa's favorite sweater?

_____

3. Who is Miss Hoover?

_____

4. What is the name of Lisa's new friend?
    a. Isabel
    b. Janine
    c. Amy
    d. Lisa

Nate Goes to the Zoo

Nate was so excited when he woke up. Today his family was going to the zoo! Nate got out of bed. He ate his breakfast. He brushed his teeth. Now he was ready to go!

"I am ready!" Nate said happily.

"Great! Let's go!" said his mom.

Nate got in the car with his mom and his dad. They drove for a long time. Finally, they arrived at the zoo.

Nate saw many animals at the zoo.

First, he saw a monkey. The monkey was swinging in a tree. The monkey was silly! Nate laughed at the monkey.

Next, Nate saw an elephant.

The elephant was very big and very tall.

Nate liked the elephant's big ears.

Last, Nate saw a lion. The lion roared.

The lion's roar was so loud!

Nate liked to roar too!

Nate felt happy to see so many animals.

Nate had so much fun at the zoo!

1. Who went with Nate to the zoo?

   _____

2. Which animal was very big and tall?

   _____

3. Which animal roared?
   a. a monkey
   b. an elephant
   c. a lion
   d. a horse

4. Did Nate have fun at the zoo?

   _____

Phoebe's Clean Teeth

Every morning and every evening,
Phoebe brushed her teeth.
She had a pink toothbrush.
She had toothpaste that tasted like mint.
Phoebe tried to do a very good job of
brushing her teeth.
One day Phoebe's mom said they were going to the dentist.
"Why do I need to visit the dentist?" asked Phoebe.
"I already keep my teeth very clean."
"The dentist will check your teeth and make sure that they are
healthy," Phoebe's mom told her.
Phoebe felt nervous about going to the dentist. Phoebe thought that
maybe it would hurt when the dentist checked her teeth.
Phoebe and her mom drove to the dentist's office. The dentist's
name was Dr. Stokes. He had a big chair in his office that Phoebe
sat in while he checked her teeth.
"Phoebe, you have very clean teeth!" exclaimed Dr. Stokes. "I can
see you do a good job brushing them."
Phoebe smiled a great big smile, showing her clean teeth to all!

1. What color was Phoebe's toothbrush?
    a. Blue
    b. Green
    c. Yellow
    d. Pink

2. When did Phoebe brush her teeth?

    _____

3. Who was Phoebe's dentist?

    _____

4. How do you think Phoebe felt at the end of the story?

    _____

The Fancy Restaurant

Steven and his family were all getting dressed in their best clothes. It was a special day. It was his parents' wedding anniversary!

To celebrate the anniversary, they were going to a restaurant. They were going to a fancy restaurant.

At the restaurant, Steven saw the waiters all wearing tuxedos. The tables of the restaurant had candles and flowers, and fancy tablecloths. Steven wasn't sure if he liked being in such a fancy place.

"I think you will like the food at the restaurant," said his dad.

"I am not sure," said Steven. "It is very fancy, and I never had fancy food before."

"It is good to try new things," said Steven's mom.

When the food arrived, Steven tasted a small bite of it. It was delicious! Steven loved the fancy food!

He ate everything on his plate!

"Happy Anniversary, Mom and Dad!"
said Steven.

"I am glad that we are celebrating
at this fancy restaurant!"

1. Why was Steven's family celebrating?
    a. It was his birthday.
    b. It was the last day of school.
    c. Dad got a new job.
    d. It was his parents' anniversary.

2. Name one thing on the tables at the restaurant.
   _____

3. What were the waiters wearing?
   _____

4. Did Steven like the fancy food?
   _____

The Secret Ingredient

Kenneth was spending the weekend at his Aunt Rose's house. He was very excited because this was a special visit. Aunt Rose promised to teach Kenneth how to bake.

Aunt Rose knew how to bake delicious desserts. Her sugar cookies and chocolate brownies always tasted so good! She also made cakes filled with cream and fruit. Kenneth wondered what kind of desserts they would bake together.

"Kenneth, we are going to bake a very special recipe," said Aunt Rose. "We are making a recipe with a secret ingredient!"

"What is it?" asked Kenneth excitedly.

"We are baking my famous banana bread!" said Aunt Rose.

Aunt Rose taught Kenneth how to mash up the bananas. She taught him how to measure the sugar and the flour. She helped him to stir it all up in a big bowl.

"And now for the secret ingredient," said Aunt Rose. "Love!" Aunt Rose gave Kenneth a big hug!

1. Where was Kenneth spending the weekend?

   _____

2. What was Aunt Rose going to teach to Kenneth?

   _____

3. What was the secret ingredient?
   a. candy
   b. love
   c. salt
   d. chocolate

4. In what kind of dish did Kenneth stir up the ingredients?

   _____

Tommy Plays Baseball

Every Saturday, Tommy went to the park. He often watched the older kids who played baseball there. Tommy wished that he could play baseball too.

Tommy asked the older kids, "Can I play baseball too?"

"No," said the older kids, "you are too young."

Tommy felt sad. He sat near the baseball field to see them play.

All of a sudden, one of the older kids hit the ball very far. It flew in the air all the way to where Tommy was sitting. Tommy jumped to his feet and caught the ball!

The whole team of older kids cheered for Tommy! They couldn't believe a younger boy could make such a great catch!

"You are a great baseball player!" they said to Tommy.

"Next Saturday, you can join the team!"

"Thanks!" said Tommy proudly.

1. Where did Tommy go on Saturdays?

   _____

2. What did Tommy wish to do?

   _____

3. Why did the older kids not let Tommy play?

   _____

4. How did Tommy show that he could play baseball with them?
   a. He threw the baseball very far.
   b. He played basketball instead.
   c. He caught the baseball.
   d. He stole their baseball.

A Feast for a King!

Ben's Uncle Felix owned a restaurant. Ben loved to go there to watch his uncle cook all the delicious food. He loved the wonderful smells coming from the restaurant's kitchen.

One evening Uncle Felix was coming to Ben's house for dinner.

"Can I help to prepare the food for Uncle Felix?" asked Ben.

"Of course," said his mother. "What should we make?"

"Let's make spaghetti with meatballs, chicken with mushrooms, and steak with potatoes!" said Ben. "Let's also make steamed vegetables with butter sauce and cookies for dessert!"

"Wow!" said his mother, "that is a lot of food!"

"Yes," said Ben, "but Uncle Felix is always cooking a lot for other people, so I want to cook a lot for him!" Ben and his mother spent the whole day preparing all the food.

When Uncle Felix arrived,
he saw all the food on the table.
"This is a feast for a king!"
exclaimed Uncle Felix.

He gave Ben a hug and sat down to eat the delicious feast!

1. Who owned a restaurant?

   _____

2. Which meal of the day was Uncle Felix going to eat at Ben's house?

   _____

3. What kind of sauce went with the steamed vegetables?

   _____

4. Why did Uncle Felix call the meal a feast for a king?
   a. The king liked spaghetti.
   b. Uncle Felix really was a king.
   c. Ben really was a king.
   d. There was so much food.

Alison's Scary Dream

Alison went to school one day. When she got there, she realized she had forgotten all of her books! The teacher was very angry with her and told her to go home.

When she returned home, she could not find her books anywhere! She looked on the table. She looked under her bed. She decided to look in the closet.

When she opened the closet door, she saw a furry creature hiding in there! It was big and had a long tail. Alison screamed!

Alison's mother ran into Alison's room.

"Wake up, Alison!" said her mother.

"You are having a scary dream!"

Her mother turned the lights on in her bedroom.

Alison opened her eyes. She saw her mother next to her bed. Alison gave her mom a big hug.

Then she told her mom all about the scary dream.

Alison felt much better after talking about it.

She realized that none of the dream was real.

Alison's mom sang her a song to comfort her.

Alison went back to bed and had no more scary dreams!

1. Why was the teacher angry?

_____

2. Name three places Alison looked for her books.

_____

3. What was in Alison's closet?
     a. her books
     b. her puppy
     c. a furry creature
     d. her brother

4. How did Alison's mom comfort her?

_____

Anthony to the Rescue!

Mrs. Jennifer lived next door to Anthony. She was a nice lady who always let Anthony come over to play with her cat, Mittens. Anthony loved playing with Mittens!

One day Mrs. Jennifer was outside looking all around.
She was very worried.
"What is wrong?" Anthony asked.
"Mittens is lost!" cried Mrs. Jennifer.
"She has been missing for an hour!"
"I will help you find her," said Anthony.
Together they looked by the flowers. Then they looked under the car. They could not find Mittens anywhere!
Suddenly Anthony heard a small sound. He followed the sound to a large apple tree behind Mrs. Jennifer's house.
"Look!" exclaimed Anthony. He pointed to a high tree branch. There was Mittens, stuck high up on the tree.
"I will help!" said Anthony. He carefully climbed into the tree. He rescued Mittens from the high tree branch!
"Thank you, Anthony!" said Mrs. Jennifer. "You saved Mittens!"

1. What kind of pet does Mrs. Jennifer have?
   a. a dog
   b. a fish
   c. a horse
   d. a cat

2. How long had Mittens been missing?

   _____

3. Where was the large apple tree?

   _____

4. Who saved Mittens?

   _____

Cleaning Day

It was a busy day. Alexander and his mom were having their weekly cleaning day! There was much to do on a cleaning day! "What should we clean first?" asked Alexander.

"Let's begin in your bedroom," said his mom. They dusted all of Alexander's shelves. They washed the sheets from his bed. They put away some of his clothes and books.

"Now, let's clean the family room," said his mom. They vacuumed the rug. They dusted the television. They washed the windows.

"Now, let's clean the kitchen," said his mom. They washed the dirty dishes. They scrubbed the pots and pans. They swept the kitchen floor.

Finally, the whole house was clean.
Alexander felt tired from all the cleaning!
He also felt proud of all the hard work
he did with his mom.
"Thank you, Alexander!" said his mom.
"You are such a big help every cleaning day!"

1. **Where did they clean first?**

_____

2. **How did they clean the rug in the family room?**

_____

3. **What did Alexander and his mom scrub?**

_____

4. **How did they clean the kitchen floor?**
   a. They vacuumed the kitchen floor.
   b. They left the kitchen floor dirty.
   c. They painted the kitchen floor.
   d. They swept the kitchen floor.

Grandpa's Boat

Ellie loved spending time at her grandparents' house.
It was near a lake. Her grandpa had a little wooden rowboat
on the lake. Her grandpa used two oars to row the boat.
In the summer, Ellie stayed at her grandparents' house. She and
her grandpa went on the boat every day. Ellie would wear a life
jacket to keep her safe while on the boat. The life jacket would
help her float in case she fell into the lake.
They would look for fish in the water. They would wave to the
other people who were in other boats. Ellie loved to go on boat
rides with her grandpa.
One time Ellie asked if she could row the boat.
"No," said her grandpa, "the oars are too heavy for you. But I
have an idea. Let's row together." Ellie sat on her grandpa's lap
and together, they used the oars to row the boat. Ellie couldn't
wait to tell her grandma that she helped to row grandpa's boat!

1. In which season did Ellie stay at her grandparents' house?

   _____

2. How did Ellie stay safe while on the boat?

   _____

3. Who went for boat rides with Ellie?

   _____

4. Why couldn't Ellie row by herself?
   a. The oars were too heavy.
   b. There were too many fish.
   c. There was a hole in the boat.
   d. She lost the oars.

The Chocolate Cake

Today was a special day.
It was Robert's dad's birthday.
Robert wanted to surprise his dad
with a special treat!
"Mom, can you help me bake a special
treat for Dad's birthday?" asked Robert.
"Yes," said his mom. "I would like to help you. What kind of treat
would you like to bake? Some cookies?"
"I would like to bake a cake!" said Robert.
"Dad loves chocolate cake!"
Robert and his mom mixed together flour, sugar, eggs, and lots of
chocolate. They put the cake into the oven for 50 minutes. The
house smelled so good while the cake was baking!
When the cake was out of the oven, Robert decorated it with
colorful candies. Robert thought that the cake looked great! He put
the cake on the table.
When Robert's dad came home from work, he was surprised! Robert
and his mom put some candles on the cake, and they sang the
Happy Birthday song.
Finally, they all ate the delicious chocolate cake!

1. Why was it a special day?

   _____

2. What kind of cake did Robert bake?

   _____

3. How long did the cake bake in the oven?

   _____

4. Where did Robert put the cake when he was done decorating it?
   a. in the closet
   b. in the oven
   c. on the table
   d. on the floor

Name:_____

The Family Reunion

The big day had finally arrived! The day of the Miller Family Reunion! Olivia, her parents, and her brothers were going to the reunion. She felt very excited!

The family reunion was at a big park. The park was a long distance from Olivia's house. It took two hours to get there!

"We are here!" Olivia's mom said happily when they arrived. Olivia saw the park was decorated with balloons and colorful streamers. There were big tables filled with lots of food.

Many of Olivia's relatives had already arrived, some of the relatives she had never met before. Olivia's mom introduced her to lots of people. There were aunts, uncles, and many cousins. Olivia met one cousin named Jane. Jane was the same age as Olivia. Jane was very nice. Olivia and Jane played many games together. They ate lots of food and had fun the whole day!

The Miller Family Reunion was wonderful. Olivia hoped that they would have another reunion next year!

1. How long did it take to get to the reunion?

   _____

2. Where was the reunion?
   a. in a forest
   b. at a beach
   c. at Grandma's house
   d. at a park

3. Who introduced Olivia to lots of people?

   _____

4. Was Jane older than Olivia, younger than Olivia, or the same age as Olivia?

   _____

The Math Test

Stella liked to read. Stella also liked to write. But Stella did not like math. She did not like working on math problems with her class! On Monday, Stella's teacher said, "On Friday, we will have a math test. Please study Chapter 7 in your math books."

"Oh no!" thought Stella. "I will fail. I do not know how to do the math. I do not understand Chapter 7."

After school, she walked home slowly. She felt worried about the math test. Stella looked very sad when she arrived home.

"What is wrong?" her mom asked.

"My class has a math test on Chapter 7, and I cannot do the math!" Stella said sadly.

"Hmm, maybe these little candies will help! We will use them to help practice doing your math problems!" said her mother.

Stella and her mother practiced all the Chapter 7 math problems using the little candies to help her count out the answers. She never knew that math could be so much fun!

On Friday, Stella took the math test. She got an A+!

"I did it!" said Stella. "Now I do like math!"

$$a = \sqrt{c^2 - b^2}$$

$$b = \sqrt{c^2 - a^2}$$

$$c = \sqrt{a^2 - b^2}$$

1. When is Stella's math test?

_____

2. Does Stella like to write?

_____

3. How did Stella's mother help?
   a. She told Stella to take a nap.
   b. She practiced with Stella by using little candies.
   c. She sang a song about math.
   d. She ate all of Stella's candies.

4. How did Stella get home from school?

_____

The Perfect Present

There was only one more day until the birthday party
for Hannah's mom. Hannah felt worried because
she still did not have a birthday present for her mom.
"I bought Mom a sweater," said her older sister.
"I bought Mom a necklace," said her older brother.
Hannah did not have much money to buy her mom a big gift.
But she still wanted to give her something special.
"Don't worry, Hannah," said her dad.
"Just give your mom something from your heart."
Hannah thought for a long time and finally decided to give her
something from her heart. She took out her crayons and some
paper. She drew a beautiful picture of her mom.
She wrote, "I love you with all my heart" on the back of the picture.
At the birthday party, Hannah's mom opened her presents.
She liked the sweater and the necklace. She loved the picture!
"This is the perfect present, Hannah!" said her mom.

1. Who bought a sweater for Hannah's mom?
   _____

2. Who bought a necklace for Hannah's mom?
   _____

3. Why couldn't Hannah buy her mom a big gift?
   a. She didn't have much money.
   b. She had too much money.
   c. She didn't like stores.
   d. She didn't like her mom.

4. What did Hannah draw?
   _____

Name:_____

The Snowy Day

Monica lived in the state of Hawaii in the United States.
In Hawaii, Monica could play outside without a coat.
There she could run in the hot sand and splash in the ocean.
In December, the family was going to visit Monica's cousin, Emily.
Emily lived in the state of Indiana. Monica was so excited.
She had never been to Indiana before!
"We will need to pack coats and hats," said Monica's mom.
"Why?" asked Monica. "Will it be cold in Indiana in December?"
"Yes! There may be snow!" said Monica's dad.
Monica could not believe it. She had never seen snow before.
When they arrived in Indiana, there was no snow.
Monica felt disappointed. On the second day in Indiana,
there was still no snow.
On the third day, Emily woke Monica up early.
"Look, Monica!" said Emily. "Look outside!"
Monica looked out the window.
Everything was covered in beautiful white snow!
It sparkled like tiny diamonds all over the ground.
Monica was so happy.
She put on her coat and went outside to play in the beautiful snow!

1. In which state did Monica live?

   _____

2. In which state did Emily live?

   _____

3. Monica's family was going to visit Emily in _____ .
      a. April   c. July
      b. October   d. December

4. Why did Monica need a coat?

   _____

   _____

I'm A Monster!

Sarah put on a mask.

She looked in the mirror and laughed at her funny clothes. This is a great outfit. Sarah ran from her bedroom into her mom and dad's room.

"ROAR! I'm coming to eat you!" she shouted.
"Wonderful costume," said mom.
"Yes, I'm a monster," Sarah replied.

1. **What was Sarah's outfit?**
   a. A witch
   b. A monster ☑
   c. An animal
   d. A fairy

2. **Where did Sarah run to?**
   a. Her brother's room
   b. The living room
   c. Her mom and dad's room ☑
   d. The kitchen

3. **Who saw Sarah?**
   Her mom ☑

4. **What did Sarah reply to her mom?**
   "Yes, I'm a monster" ☑

First Boat Ride

Angie and her mom are going on a boat trip. Angie's mom drives to the port.

"This is my first time on a boat!"
Angie tells the crew member and the captain.

"Welcome aboard," says the captain.
"Have a great trip," says the crew member.

Angie and her mom sit down and look out of the window. The boat starts to move. Angie and her mom go for a walk on the boat's deck. Angie can feel the wind on her face as the boat sails across the water. They can see houses and shops next to the water. People wave as the boat passes. They see fish in the water.

"I think I love boat rides; they are fun!" Angie says to mom.

1. **Who drives to the port?** Angie's mom ☑

2. **Who says "Welcome aboard," to Angie?**
   a. The captain ☑   b. Angie's mom
   c. Angie's dad   d. The waiter

3. **What can Angie and her mom see in the water?**
   Fish ☑

4. **What does Angie think of this boat's ride?**
   a. Great   b. Boring   c. Slow   d. Fun ☑

The New Pencil Case

Carl's pencil case had scratches on it. It had a small dent too. He wanted a nice new pencil case. Carl asked dad,
"Please can I have a new pencil case?"
"I'm sorry, son, but your old pencil case is still good for now," dad said. Carl was sad. He thought for a few minutes.
"Perhaps I can buy my own new pencil case.
How much will it cost?"
"Around three dollars," dad replied.

Carl went to the playroom and got his money box. He carefully counted all of his coins, but he had only one dollar.
"I need to make more money!" thought Carl.

Carl thought and thought of different ways to get his new pencil case but he had no ideas. A few days later at school, Carl came top in his math test. His teacher gave him a sticker of a dinosaur. Carl stuck the sticker on his pencil case.

Carl did well in his schoolwork all week and got lots of stickers at school. He put them all on his pencil case. He then realized that he could use his one dollar to buy more stickers. He bought more stickers from the shop and completely covered his old pencil case. It looked like a new pencil case. All of the scratches were covered. Carl was happy with his pencil case.

1. **How much would a new pencil case cost?**
   Around three dollars ☑

2. **Which subject of school test did Carl come top in?**
   Math test ☑

3. **What was the first sticker Carl put on his pencil case?**
   a. Dinosaur ☑ b. Dragon   c. Bird   d. Dog

4. **Which room did Carl keep his money-box?**
   Playroom ☑

Garden

Jordan and Lee were sitting in the garden. They were looking around at all plants, nature, and insects. They could see many interesting things.

Jordan saw a pretty flower.
"Look at that beautiful pink flower," Jordan said.
"That is not a flower," Lee said. "It's food for butterflies."

A butterfly came and landed on the flower and sipped the sweet nectar. Then, Jordan saw a small brown twig.
"Look at that twig," said Jordan.
"That is not a twig," Lee replied.
"It's a building block for a bird's house."

Birds swooped down and picked up the little twig. They flew up on the tree and build their nest. Jordan saw a leaf.
"Look at that green leaf," Jordan said.
"That is not a leaf. It's a shady umbrella for beetles," Lee said.

A beetle crawled under the large leaf to escape from the sunshine. The garden is full of many useful things for nature!

1. **Who are the two boys in the story?**
   Jordan and Lee ☑

2. **What was the second thing Jordan saw?**
   A small brown twig ☑

3. **What did Lee say about leaf?**
   It's a shady umbrella for beetles ☑

4. **What color was the flower?** Pink ☑

Sounds

He listened. These sounds were what he heard:
Children laughed as they played outside. His brother played soft music on the piano in the dining room. A door creaked.

A telephone rang shrilly somewhere in the house. The kettle bubbled and hissed as it boiled. His watch was ticking.

A van rumbled down the street. The washing machine whirred. Outside, a bird shrieked loudly. His cat purred in contentment.

The wind howled and whooshed. Somebody was using a lawnmower to cut their grass. The pages of his book quietly rustled as he turned a new page to read more.

1. **Which room was the piano in?**
   Dining room ☑

2. **Fill in the blanks:**
   A ☑(van) rumbled down the street.
   The washing machine ____(whirred)☑.
   ☑(Outside) , a bird shirked ____(loudly)☑.
   His cat ☑(purred) in contentment.
   The wind howled and ____(whooshed)☑ .

3. **What was the creaking sound from?** A door ☑

4. **Where did the children play?**
   Outside ☑

The Storm

The duck waddled quickly to the field, happy to have a picnic with her farmyard friends. She stopped and looked up. Big gray clouds filled the sky. She thought a storm was coming. Frightened, Duck started to hurry back to the barn.

She passed Chicken, Goat, and Sheep. "Why aren't you going to the field for our picnic?" Chicken asked. "I think the rain is coming. We should stay safe inside," Duck replied. Sheep looked at the clouds in the sky. "I think it will be fine. It doesn't look too bad," Sheep said. Duck still wasn't sure. "Up to you," Goat said. "We are still going to have fun at the picnic." The three friends left.

As Duck got closer to the barn, she also passed Pig, Horse, and Cow. All animals were excited about the picnic. The duck was happy to reach the shelter of the barn. She was worried about her friends, though.

Suddenly, thunder crashed in the air. Lightning bolts lit up the sky. The barn shook. Big drops of rain started to fall from the storm clouds. Duck looked outside. Her friends were running back to the barn. The ground outside was quickly muddy. The wind howled.

As the other farm animals charged into the barn, they moaned. "You were right!" Horse said. "We are so cold and wet!" Duck smiled. She was happy her friends were safe. They could have a picnic

1. **What were three animals the duck see first?**
   Chicken, goat and sheep ☑

2. **Which place did their friends plan to have a picnic?** ☑
   a. at the farm   b. in the barn   c. in the forest   d. in the field

3. **What crashed in the air?** Thunder ☑

4. **Why did Duck smile?**
   She was happy that her friends were safe. ☑

Wake Up

"I'm so sleepy today," said Rooster.
"I don't know if I will wake up on time in the morning."

"Don't worry," Cow said. "I'll moo very loudly to wake you."
"Who will wake you?" Rooster asked, worried.

"I'll wake Cow," Sheep said.
"I'll do my biggest baaaaa."

"But, who will wake you?"

"I'll wake Sheep," Pig said. "I'll grunt and oink like she's never heard before. But, someone must wake me first!"

"I'll wake Pig. I'll howl and bark until his eyes fly open," said Dog. "How will you wake up?" asked Sheep.

"No problem," said Dog.
"I always wake up as soon as I hear Rooster shout."

"What a good plan!" said Rooster as he started to laugh.

1. **How does Rooster feel at the start of the story?**
   Sleepy ☑

2. **Who will wake Sheep?**
   Pig ☑

3. **How will Dog wake Pig?**
   Howl and bark ☑

4. **Fill in the gaps:**
   "What a ____(good)☑ plan!" said ____(Rooster)☑ as he
   started to ____(laugh)☑

The Missing Gloves

Grandma looked at the coat rack with a frown.
"My gloves aren't here," she said.
"Okay, Grandma, what are your gloves like?" Margie asked.
"They thick and brown," Grandma replied.
"When did you last wear them?" Brett asked.
"I wore them when I walked to the shop this morning. Then, I came back and hung them on the coat rack with my coat and scarf. They should be here, but they're not." Grandma said.
"Here are some gloves," Margie said. "But they are blue."
"No, they are Grandpa's gloves," Grandma said, still frowning.
"Here are some red gloves," Brett said.
"They are mine," said Margie.
"We need to look for brown gloves."
They looked in Grandma's coat pocket. There were no gloves. They looked on the floor. They looked behind the sofa. They looked in the kitchen. They could not find any brown gloves. Right then, Grandpa came through the door.
"Hi Grandpa, where did you go?" asked Brett.
"I took the dog for a walk in the park," Grandpa said.
"It's cold outside today!"
Margie started to giggle. "I know where your gloves are, Grandma. Look at Grandpa's hands." Grandpa was wearing thick, brown gloves.
"My gloves!" shouted Grandma. "Sorry, I didn't think you needed them, and they are warmer than mine," Grandpa said sheepishly.
"It's okay," said Grandma. "Now I can go and visit our neighbor with warm hands. Thank you for helping me look for my gloves, children."

1. **What was the color of Margie's gloves?** Red ☑
2. **Where did Grandpa go?**
   a. To the shop   b. To a restaurant
   c. To visit a friend   d. To the park ☑
3. **Who helped Grandma look for her gloves?**
   Margie and Brett ☑
4. **Who had Grandma's gloves?** Grandpa ☑

Clouds

Charlotte and her cousin, Jim,
were sitting outside in the garden.

There were many white,
fluffy clouds in the blue sky.

"Look," Charlotte pointed to the sky,
"What do you think that cloud looks like?"
"It looks like a clown," said Jim. "A clown cloud!"
"To me, it looks like a dragon," Charlotte said. "How about
   that one?" Charlotte pointed to a different cloud.
"I think it looks like an elf," said Jim.
"Hmmm. To me, it looks like a fairy," said Charlotte.

The two cousins continued looking at the shapes of the clouds.
"Oh no," said Charlotte as she pointed to a big gray cloud.
"What about that one?" Jim replied, "It looks like a duck."
"To me, it looks like rain!" Charlotte laughed.
A fat raindrop fell from the sky and plopped on the ground.
Then they ran back into the house.

1. **What is the relationship between Charlotte
   and Jim?** _____ Cousins ☑

2. **What does Charlotte think the first cloud
   looks like?** Dragon ☑

3. **What does Jim think the gray cloud looks like?**
   Duck ☑

4. **Why did Charlotte and Jim run into the house?**
   It started to rain ☑

Bedtime Story

Willow loved listening to stories at bedtime. Willow's mom reads
her a bedtime story every night. Sometimes the stories were
about magical lands. Sometimes, they were about children.
Some stories were about animals. Sometimes, she told stories
about the holidays. Mom's bedtime stories are always fun!

Willow was excited about mom's newest story. But today, when
bedtime comes, Dad takes Willow up to bed instead. He tucks
her into bed and kisses her head.
   "What about my story?" Willow asked.
   "Tonight Mom is busy," Dad said. "Your little sister is sick.
   But I can read you a bedtime story."
Dad tells a wonderful story about fairies and elves, unicorns,
and animals. Willow falls asleep happy, thinking of a fairytale
land.

1. **Who always told Willow a bedtime story?**
   Mom ☑

2. **Who is sick?** Her little sister ☑

3. **What does Dad tell Willow about story?
   (Complete the blank spaces)**

   Fairies and   [elves]☑ unicorns, and   [animals]☑.

4. **What is Willow thinking about when
   she falls asleep?**
      a. Her mom and dad   b. A fairytale land ☑
      c. Dragons   d. School work

New Dress

Melanie loved her new dress.
It was a cool summer dress.
It was her favorite color pink.
It had lots of small flowers on it too.
And, best of all, it had two cute pockets.

It had hung in her closet for several weeks. She had waited for
the spring getting warmer and the blooming flowers.

Then, the sun was shining, and birds sang on the green trees.
Butterflies flitted between the flowers. It was a warm day.

Melanie could wear her new dress! She put on her new dress
and went to play in the park with her friends.

1. **What was Melanie's new item of clothing?**
      a. Dress ☑
      b. Shoes
      c. Skirt
      d. Coat

2. **What is Melanie's favorite color?**
   Pink ☑

3. **What were birds doing on the trees?**
      a. Singing ☑
      b. Eating
      c. Sleeping
      d. Flying

4. **Where did Melanie go?**
   Park ☑

Sunshine

One hot, sunny day, Dad picked up Danielle from school.
When they arrived home, they went inside. It was cool
because Dad put the air conditioning on.
   "Today, it is too hot. I'm tired of the sun. I can't wait for the
   cooler winter," said Dad.
He sat down in the cool living room with a cold glass of water.
   "I love the sunshine!" Danielle smiled. "I think I'll go and play
   with my friends for some time."
Danielle changed her clothes and ran outside. She met her
friend's, Michelle and Debbie. They had fun outside in the sun.

They played jump rope. They threw the ball. They splashed
water from the fountain. They sat in the shade of a tree and
talked about pop music. Then, they all started to feel hot.
Danielle went home. She walked into the house, hot and
sweaty. The air conditioning made her felt great!
   "Here, drink this," Mom said. She gave Danielle a glass of
   chilled lemonade.
   "Mmmm, I like lemonade," said Danielle as she took a big
   gulp and smiled.

1. **Who picked up Danielle from school?**
   Dad ☑

2. **What did dad drink?**
   Water ☑

3. **What did Danielle drink?**
   Lemonade ☑

4. **What were Danielle's friends' names?**
   Michelle and Debbie ☑

Thai Islands

It was Carl's first time on the Thai Islands. His family had taken a vacation to a big island called Koh Samui. They were so many things to enjoy. Carl was amazed.

"Let's swim in the sea!" Carl shouted to his brother.
They ran into the soft waves, that the water was clear and cold.
"Now let's hunt for seashells," Carl said.
They walked along the sand, picking up colorful shells.

"Let's play Frisbee!" Carl said.
They threw the Frisbee back and forward to each other and ran on the soft, white sand.

"Now let's build a sandcastle," Carl said.
They dug a moat and collected buckets of sand to make a big, grand castle on the beach. Carl and his brother had a great day at the beach on the Thai Islands.

1. Which Thai Island did Carl visit? Koh Samui ☑

2. What did Carl and his brother play with?
   a. A ball   b. An inflatable toy
   c. A kite   d. A Frisbee ☑

3. What did the two brothers make on the beach?
   Sandcastle ☑

4. What color is the sand on the island?
   White ☑

Spider Web

Mary was playing in the garden with her sister, Florence. She ran through a big spider's web by accident.

The sticky web stuck to her face and hair. She hopped and jumped, yelling. She quickly wiped her face and hair. Mary was scared of spiders!

"A spider! A spider's web! Where is it? Get the spider off me!" Mary rubbed her face and hair some more. She felt the sticky web on her fingertips.

"I can feel it! It's huge! The spider is on me," Mary screamed in horror.
"Can you find the spider?" She asked Florence.

Florence laughed. "I think that's the spider," Florence said as she pointed to the tree trunk. A small spider ran up the trunk and onto a leaf.

1. What is Mary's sister called?
   Florence ☑

2. How did the web feel?
   a. Slimy   b. Sloppy
   c. Sticky ☑   d. Soft

3. What did the spider run onto?
   Leaf ☑

4. Why was Mary upset?
   Because she's scared of spiders ☑

Carrot Cake

Wanda's school is having a cake sale.

What should Wanda take?
Chocolate brownies?
Lemon muffins?

Wanda looks in the kitchen cupboards. She thinks long and hard. She asks Mom for ideas.

"Mom, we have a cake sale at school. What can I make?"
Mom thinks too. "Shall we make a carrot cake?"
"That's a fantastic idea!" Wanda says happily.

Wanda and Mom bake a delicious carrot cake. All of Wanda's classmates love the tasty cake.

1. Who helps Wanda to making a cake?
   Mom ☑

2. What kind of cake that Wanda make?
   Carrot cake ☑

3. Why does Wanda want to make a cake?
   a. For a cake sale at school ☑
   b. For her friend's birthday
   c. For a party at Girl Scouts
   d. For a bake sale at her club

4. What does Wanda think of making before Mom had an idea? (Complete the spaces)
   [chocolate] ☑ brownies or   [lemon] ☑ muffins.

The Fox

One afternoon I saw something in the bushes. It was a small fox. It ran right past me. I wanted to see where it was going, so I chased after it.

The fox ran quickly. It was difficult to see. I ran faster. It ran behind a tree, through a bush. I could not find it.

Suddenly, I saw it again. It moved quickly. It was the fox! It ran into a hole. I ran towards the hole then hid behind a bush. I watched the fox come out of the hole with her baby foxes. They ate and played.

1. What kind of animal was in the story?
   Fox ☑

2. What did the fox run through?
   Bushes ☑

3. What did the fox run into?
   Hole ☑

4. What did the fox and her baby foxes do?
   Ate and played ☑

Akash and Sarah

Akash and Sarah were playing on the beach.
They ran across the soft sand and paddled in the sea.
 "Let's collect some seashells," Sarah said to Akash.
 "Okay, I'd love to," Akash said.
They walked up and down the beach, picking up a beautiful collection of shells.
 "I know," Sarah said. "Let's build a big sandcastle and cover it with our shells."
 "What a great idea," Akash said.
So they collected buckets of sand, dug a hole for the moat, and filled it with water. When their sandcastle was finished, they carefully decorated it with their shells. Akash picked up a stick.
 "I'm going to draw a heart around our castle."
 "What a lovely idea," Sarah said.
They both smiled at their castle covered with shells and a big, beautiful heart.

1. **What are the names of the two friends?**
   Akash and Sarah ✓

2. **Where were they playing?**
   On the beach ✓

3. **What did they build?**
   A sandcastle ✓

4. **What did Akash draw with a stick?**
   a. Butterfly   b. Castle
   c. Flower   d. Heart ✓

Sock Puppets

Ella, her sister Marie, and Grandma sat on the sofa.
 "What shall we do tonight?" Ella asked.
 "I know! Let's have a puppet show!" Marie said excitedly.
 "But how?" asked Ella. "We haven't got any puppets."
 "We can make them!" Marie said as she ran out of the room. She came back with the laundry basket and Grandma's sewing box.
 "We can make faces on the socks!" Marie laughed.
So they each took a clean sock and sewed buttons for the eyes. They then stitched mouths on the socks with red cotton.
Marie put a sock over her hand, opened and closed her hand. The sock puppet looked like it was talking.
 "Hello, I'm a baby sock," Marie giggled.
Ella laughed and grabbed her sock.
 "Hi, I'm daddy sock."
They all laughed. Grandma made a deep voice and said, "Hello baby and daddy sock. I'm Grandpa sock."
Everyone laughed as they created their own sock puppet play. It was a fun evening.

1. **Who suggested having a puppet show?** Marie ✓

2. **What did they use for eyes?** Buttons ✓

3. **Complete the blank spaces:**
   Grandma made a   [deep] ✓ voice and said,
   " [Hello] ✓ baby and   [daddy] ✓ sock.
   I'm   [Grandpa] ✓ sock."

4. **What did Marie call her sock puppet?**
   a. Mommy sock   b. Baby sock ✓
   c. Grandma sock   d. Sister sock

The Funfair

At the weekend, Martha went to the funfair with her mom and dad. There were so many things to do! There were stalls selling cotton candy and ice cream, a small petting zoo, rides, and games. Martha raced around in the bumper cars and rode a fast roller coaster. She felt as though she was going into the clouds!

After the rides, Martha came to a games stand. She wanted to throw the small balls to knock over tin cans. The stall owner told her if she could knock down five cans she would win a prize. Martha looked at the prizes—there was a giant, colorful unicorn. She dearly wanted it. Martha aimed and threw with all of her power.
One can fell. Only four more!
Martha threw the rest of the balls and won her prize. She hugged her new unicorn all the way home.

1. **Where did Martha go with her mom and dad?**
   a. The park   b. The zoo
   c. The funfair ✓   d. The supermarket

2. **What rides did Martha go on?**
   Bumper cars and roller coaster ✓

3. **How many cans did Martha need to knock down to win a prize?** 5 ✓

4. **What did Martha get for a prize?**
   Unicorn ✓

Pepper Seeds

Barbara's mom gave her two pepper plant seeds.
 "I want to see them grow," Barbara said.
 "Seeds need water and sunlight to grow," her mom said.
They planted the seeds in a jar, watered them, and placed them on the window ledge. The sunlight came through the window and warmed the jar. In a few days, the seeds had started to sprout. Barbara was excited.
 "Look, mom! My pepper seeds are growing!"
 "If you take good care of them, they will continue to grow," mom said. "Make sure they have enough water and don't move them from the sunlight."
The seedlings continued to grow. Barbara was happy.
 "I helped the seeds to grow. I gave them everything they needed."

1. **How many pepper seeds did Barbara have?**
   2 ✓

2. **What two things do seeds need to grow?**
   Water and sunlight ✓

3. **Where did Barbara put her jar on?**
   Window ledge ✓

4. **Complete the blank spaces:**
   Barbara was   [happy] ✓. "I helped the   [seeds] ✓
   to grow. I   [gave] ✓ them   [everything] ✓ they
   needed."

Pets

Name:_____

Many people have pets. Some people have dogs as pets. Others have cats. Some people have fish, turtles or rabbits.

Grandpa is not like most people. His three pets are hamsters. They are all girls. One is called Kylie, one is called Kay and the other is called

1. **How many pets does Grandpa have?**
   3 ☑

2. **What animals does Grandpa have?**
   Hamsters ☑

3. **Is Kay a boy or a girl?**
   Girl ☑

4. **Fill in the spaces:**
   Some people have ___[dogs]☑ as pets. Others have [cats]☑. Some people have [fish]☑, turtles or rabbits.

The Ring

Name:_____

Joanne found a ring.
Whose ring is it?

Is it Shelley's ring?
No. Shelley's ring is silver.
This ring is gold.

Is it Debbie's ring?
No. Debbie's ring has a big pink stone.
This ring has a big blue stone.

Is it Sharon's ring?
No. Sharon's ring has small purple stones.
This ring has small yellow stones.

Joanne did not know what to do with the ring.
Just then, Paula walked into the classroom.
"Oh, my ring!" cried Paula. "I'm so happy you found it!"

Joanne was happy to find the ring's owner.
Paula was happy to have her ring back.

1. **Who found a ring?**
   Joanne ☑

2. **Whose ring has a big pink stone?**
   Debbie ☑

3. **What was Paula happy about?**
   To have her ring back ☑

4. **Where did Joanne and Paula see each other?**
   Classroom ☑

What is It?

Name:_____

Shona was sleepy. She went upstairs to her bedroom.
It was time for bed. She brushed her teeth, changed into her pajamas, and climbed into bed.
She snuggled underneath her duvet.

Suddenly, she heard her door quietly creaking open.
It was dark and she couldn't see what made the sound.
She called to her sister,
   "Sophie! Is that you?" There was no reply.
She shouted to her brother,
   "Toby, are you there?"
Again, there was no reply. Then, something jumped onto her bed. It jumped across her and licked her face.
Shona giggled. It was Fluff, her playful puppy.

1. **What did Shona brush?**
   a. Her hair   b. Her puppy
   c. Her clothes   d. Her teeth ☑

2. **What sound did the door make?**
   a. Squeak   b. Creak ☑
   c. Groan   d. Bang

3. **What is Shona's brother called?**
   Toby ☑

4. **What jumped on Shona's bed?**
   Toby – her puppy ☑

My White Dog

Name:_____

I have a pet dog.
She is big and white.
She is called Marley.

We play with a stick. I throw a stick for Marley.
She runs after it and brings it back to me.

I throw the stick again.
It goes into the pond.
Marley splashes in the water to fetch the stick.
She brings it back.

1. **What color is Marley?**
   White ☑

2. **What does Marley play with?**
   A stick ☑

3. **Where does the stick go?**
   Into the pond ☑

4. **What does Marley do with the pond?**
   She splashes into the water. ☑

My Playful Kitten

My kitten is very playful. She loves to play with everything. She plays with toy mice, balls, bells and string.

My kitten found a ball of yarn. It was white. My kitten pulled and chased the yarn.

My kitten found a ball. It was red. She rolled the ball underneath the sofa.

My kitten found a toy mouse. It was blue. She chewed the toy mouse.

My kitten found a bell. It was yellow. She made lots of noise with the bell. My kitten is now very tired!

1. **What color was the toy mouse?**
   Blue ✓

2. **What did the kitten pull and chase?**
   Ball of yarn ✓

3. **What was red?**
   A ball ✓

4. **What did the kitten make lots of noise with?**
   A bell ✓

Barbecue

Lenny walked into the back garden with his dad. He helped his dad pile coals on the grill and watched his dad start the fire. The coals began to smoke.

Mom carried out a tray of meat. Dad put the food on the barbecue. The smell was delicious! Lenny sniffed and inhaled the tempting smells. "Yum!"

Their pet dog ran over, wagging his tail. "Woof!" "I think someone else is excited for BBQ, too!" laughed Lenny. "It won't be long," dad said. "Help mom bring the salad and bread to the table."

Lenny and the dog ran into the kitchen. The dog picked up his ball and looked at Lenny. Lenny played with his dog. He forgot what his dad asked him to do.

"BBQ time!" shouted dad. Lenny ran to the garden. There was no salad. There was no bread. He quickly ran back to the kitchen to help mom. He was excited to eat the delicious grilled meats.

1. **Who started the fire?** Dad ✓

2. **What two things did Lenny need to take to the table for mom?** Salad and bread ✓

3. **Fill in the black spaces:**
   Lenny and the [dog]✓ ran into the [kitchen]✓ The dog picked up his [ball]✓ and looked at Lenny. Lenny [played]✓ with his dog. He [forgot]✓ what his dad asked him to do.

4. **What was Lenny excited to eat?** Grilled meats ✓

Harvest Time

Sophie and Grandpa planted seeds in the garden. They wanted to grow their own fresh vegetables.

Sophie and Grandpa waited for the plants to grow. When the time passed, they watered the seedlings and made sure the birds couldn't eat them.
   "When can we pick the radishes?" Sophie asked.
   "Tomorrow," replied Grandpa.
   "When can we pick the carrots?" Sophie asked.
   "Tomorrow," replied Grandpa.
   "When can we pick the peas?" Sophie asked.
   "Tomorrow," replied Grandpa.

Sophie waited for the sun to shine down on her garden the next day. She wore her old clothes and put on her gardening gloves.
   "Grandpa! It's time!" Sophie called out in excitement. Together, Sophie and Grandpa harvested their vegetables. They picked radishes, carrots, and peas. They were both happy with their garden.

1. **Who did Sophie plant seeds with?** Grandpa ✓

2. **What seeds did Sophie plant?**
   Radishes, carrots, and peas ✓

3. **When did Grandpa say they could harvest the vegetables?**
   a. Today   b. Saturday
   c. Thursday   d. Tomorrow ✓

4. **How did Sophie and Grandpa feel at the end of the story?** Happy ✓

Lunch Time

Rana's mom is making lunch. She is making vegetable pasta, garlic bread, and salad. Rana and her sister, Betty, want to help.

Rana put cucumber in the salad. She spread garlic butter on the bread.

Betty washed lettuce leaves for the salad. She set the table. When lunch was ready, they called their brother and dad.

   "Martin! Dad! Lunch is ready!"

Martin and dad washed their hands and sat at the table. The family enjoyed a delicious lunch together.

When everyone finished eating Dad, and Martin washed the dishes. Rana, Betty, and Mom sat in the garden

1. **Which meal was Mom making?**
   Lunch ✓

2. **What did Rana put in the salad?**
   a. Cucumber ✓
   b. Carrot
   c. Lettuce
   d. Tomato

3. **Who set the table?**
   Betty ✓

4. **Who washed the dishes?**
   Dad and Martin ✓

A Cold Day in Winter

We get ready for school. It's cold outside, so we dress warmly.
We wear our winter coats, scarves, gloves, and hats over our
school uniform.

We drink hot chocolate before we leave the house.
The wind blows coldly around us as we wait for the school bus.
We can see our breath in the icy air.

The blue bus drives towards us.
"Get on, it's cold outside today!" the driver says.
We sit down on the bus. At outside, the trees have no leaves.
There's snow on the ground. The road is slippery.

The bus is nice and warm. We arrive at school.
We shiver as we get off the bus. The path is slippery.
We walk as fast as we can to our warm classroom.

We take off our coats, scarves, gloves, and hats.
We blow on our hands to warm them up.
Our classroom is nice and warm. Our teacher is happy.

1. **What is the weather like outside?** Cold ✓
2. **What color is the school bus?** Blue ✓
3. **How do the bus and classroom feel?**
   Nice and warm ✓
4. **Fill in the blank spaces:**
   We arrive at [school]✓. We shiver as we get off
   the [bus]✓. The path is [slippery]✓. We walk
   as fast as we can to our warm [classroom]✓.
   We take off our [coats]✓, scarves, [gloves]✓,
   and hats. We blow on our [hands]✓ to warm
   them up.

The Best

Tom and Tim are brothers. Tom is slow and careful.
Tim is quick and always wants to be the first.
He thinks that being first is the best.
   "I can eat my dinner quicker. I am the best!" Tim said.
   "I taste my food and eat slower. I don't care about
   being first. I want to enjoy my meal." Tom said.
   "I can finish my school work first. I am the best!" Tim said.
   "I don't care about being first," Tom replied.
   "I want to do my work well."
   "I can run up the stairs quicker. I am the best!" Tim said.
   "I don't want to fall down.
   I am happy to be careful." Tom said.
Tim rushed to zip up his jacket. He hurried so much the zip got
stuck. He couldn't fasten up his jacket to go to school.

Tom looked. "It would help if you slowed down," he said.
He carefully helped Tim to free the zip.
   "Thank you, Tom," Tim said. "You're the best!"

1. **Which brother wants to be the best?**
   Tim ✓
2. **What can Tim run up quicker?**
   The stairs ✓
3. **What does Tom want to enjoy?**
   His meal ✓
4. **What part of jacket does Tim have problems with?**
   Zip ✓

Twins

Lee and Lisa are brother and sister. They are twins.
They look very alike. They have very different personalities,
though. They are very different people.

Lee loves to eat sweet food, like cake and chocolate.
Lisa prefers savory food, like pizza and chips.

Lee's favorite subject in school is art.
Lisa's favorite subject is sport.

Lee likes comic books.
Lisa likes storybooks.

Lee's favorite color is green.
Lisa's favorite color is purple.

Lee is quiet and shy.
Lisa is loud and talkative.

There are many differences between the twins.
They look alike on the outside, but inside they are different.
They are still best friends though, and love each other lots.

1. **What are the names of the twins?**
   Lee and Lisa ✓
2. **What kind of books does Lee like?**
   Comic books ✓
3. **Whose favorite color is purple?**
   Lisa ✓
4. **Which twin is shy?**
   Lee ✓

Games

Charlie and Phoebe are playing games at home.
They decide to play hide and seek. Charlie closes his eyes
and counts 1 to 50. Phoebe runs to hide.
   "Ready or not, here I come!" Charlie shouts.
He looks in the living room. He looks behind the sofa.
He looks under the table. He looks behind the table, but
still cannot find Phoebe.

Charlie goes into the hall. He cannot see Phoebe.
He goes into the kitchen. He looks behind the door.
   "Found you!" He shouts. But it is a cat.
   "Found you!" He opens the cupboard quickly,
   but he only finds snacks.
Then, he hears a quiet giggle. He watches the cat walk to
the side of the washing machine. He follows the cat.
He finds Phoebe curled up in a small space between the
wall and the washing machine.
   "Found you!" He shouts.

1. **Which room does Charlie look for her first?**
   a. Living room ✓   b. Dining room
   c. Kitchen   d. Bedroom
2. **What is Charlie's friend called?**
   Phoebe ✓
3. **What does Charlie find behind the kitchen door?**
   The cat ✓
4. **What is the word does Charlie shout?**
   "Found you!" ✓

Play Time

"Can we play a game?" Lucy asked her brother Ben.
"Even though I'm bored, I need to do my math homework.
Maybe later." Ben replied.

"OK. I have an idea. I'm your teacher!" Lucy said.
"Open your math book." Ben opened his book.
"Sharpen your pencil," Lucy said. Ben sharpened his pencil.

"Now take your exercise book out of your bag. Open a new
page and write the date at the top. Draw a line under the
date." Ben did what Lucy told him to.

"Now, read the problems and write the answers in your
exercise book." Lucy watched as Ben completed his
homework.

When he had finished, Lucy said, "Now, close your books
and put them back in your bag." Ben smiled. "Thank you
Lucy. You helped me to do my homework." Lucy laughed.
"No, we played a game!"

1. **Who wanted to play?** Lucy ☑

2. **What homework did Ben do?** Math ☑

3. **What did Ben write first at the top of the page?**
   The date ☑

4. **Where did Ben put his books when he finished
   his homework?**
   a. On his desk   b. In his bag ☑
   c. On a shelf   d. In his cupboard

Vampire Cat

After lunch, Mom said to Kayla,
   "Let's rearrange and tidy your bedroom."
   "Yes," said Kayla. "Oscar can help as well." Kayla said to
her cat.
Kayla called her cat, but he didn't come.
   "Oscar! Oscar! Where are you?"
   "Do you know where Oscar is?" Kayla asked Mom.
   "I'm not sure. I did see him in my bedroom this
morning, though." Mom replied.
   "I'll go and look for him," Kayla said.

She went into Mom's bedroom and called her cat.
   "Oscar! Come here boy." She couldn't see Oscar.

She pulled back the blanket on Mom's bed. Oscar was
underneath, curled up. The sheet was draped over his
head like a cloak. He looked like a vampire!
   "Oh, Oscar. There you are! You look just like a vampire.
I think that's what you should be at a costume party!"

1. **What room did Kayla and Mom plan to
   rearrange and tidy?** Bedroom ☑

2. **What kind of animal is Oscar?**
   Cat ☑

3. **What room did Kayla find Oscar in?**
   Mom's bedroom ☑

4. **What did Oscar look like?**
   a. Vampire ☑ b. Turtle   c. Ghost   d. Postman

Collections

Charlotte and her brother Max are at the beach.

Charlotte likes to collect seashells. She thinks the seashells
are beautiful. She walks along the beach, looking for pretty
shells. Max follows her.

Charlotte picks up a shell.
   "Oh, there's a crab under this shell," Charlotte shouts.
Charlotte picks up another shell.
   "Oh, there's so much sand on this shell," Charlotte says.
Charlotte walks over to another shell.
   "Oh, there's another crab!" she screams.
Charlotte continues to look for pretty seashells.
Max keeps following her.
   "Max, why are you right behind me?
   Why are you following me?"
Max laughed. He showed her inside his bucket.
   "I'm collecting crabs!"

1. **What is under the third shell that
   Charlotte picks up?** Crab ☑

2. **What is Charlotte's brother called?**
   Max ☑

3. **What is Max collecting?**
   Crabs ☑

4. **Where does this story take place?**
   At the beach ☑

Lunch Time

Marie and Anda sit down to eat lunch together.

   "What's in your lunch box?" Marie asks Anda.
   "I have a cheese sandwich today. I also have
   orange juice and an apple." Anda replied.
   "What's in your lunch box?" Anda asks Marie.
   "I have a ham sandwich. I have a bottle of water
   and yogurt as well." Marie replied.

They both enjoy their lunch together.

1. **Who has an apple in the lunch box?**
   Anda ☑

2. **Who has a yogurt?**
   Marie ☑

3. **What kind of sandwich does Marie have?**
   Ham ☑

4. **Which meal are the two friends eating?**
   Lunch ☑

Making Pizza

"What are you doing?" Tony asked his big sister Joy.
"I'm making a pizza," Joy replied.
"Can I help?" asked Tony.
"Sorry, no. You're too small to make pizza," Joy told him.

Tony watched as Joy mixed flour, water, salt, and yeast together to make the pizza base.

He watched her chop vegetables to put on top of the pizza. She chopped onions, tomatoes, and peppers. She also had a jar of olives.

Joy spread tomato paste on the pizza base. She was about to sprinkle the toppings on top.
"Wait a moment!" Tony shouted.
He ran to the refrigerator. "You forgot the cheese!"
"Ah, thank you," Joy said. I guess you're not too little to help after all!"

1. **Complete the blank spaces:**

   He watched her chop ___[vegetables]✓__ to put on top of the ___[pizza]✓__. She chopped ___[onions]✓__, tomatoes, and ___[peppers]✓__. She also had a jar of olives.

2. **What is Joy mixing with flour, water, salt, and yeast for?** Pizza base ✓

3. **What did Joy forget?**
   Cheese ✓

4. **What is the relation between Tony to Joy?**
   Brother and sister ✓

Family Dinner

The Jones family was eating dinner together.

Around the table were Mom and Dad and their three children, Terry, Sandra, and Paul.

   "Thanks, Mom. That was delicious!"

Sandra said when they finished eating.
   "Yes, thanks, Mom. What's for dessert?" Terry asked.
   "Chocolate brownie with ice cream. You can choose chocolate, vanilla, or strawberry ice cream," Mom replied.
   "Yum! I'll have chocolate ice cream, please!" Terry said.
   "Can I have strawberry, please?" Sandra asked.
   "And, all three flavors for me, please!" Paul laughed.

1. **What are Sandra's two brothers called?**
   Terry, Paul ✓

2. **What is for dessert?**
   Chocolate brownie with ice cream ✓

3. **Who wants all three flavors of ice cream?**
   Paul ✓

4. **What flavor ice cream does Terry want?**
   Chocolate ✓

The Pet Shop

Mom and Dad took Sally and James to the pet shop.
There were many animals. There were puppies, kittens, rabbits, hamsters, mice, fish, birds, lizards, snakes, and more.

James wanted to get a mouse.
   "We are not getting a mouse, they scare me," Mom said.

Sally wanted to get a puppy.
   "We are not getting a puppy.
   They need too much time and money," Dad said.

They thought about getting a kitten or a hamster.
They knew they could only have one pet.

Eventually, Sally and James agreed to get a rabbit.
They are cute and friendly. They chose a small brown rabbit and called her Floppy.

1. **Where did Mom and Dad take their two children?**
   Pet shop ✓

2. **Why didn't Mom want a mouse?**
   They scare her ✓

3. **What color is the new pet?**
   Brown ✓

4. **What kind of animal is Floppy?**
   Rabbit ✓

School work

Carol and Alice are doing their school homework together.

Carol loves math, and Alice loves art. Alice has ten math questions to do. Carol helps Alice with her math homework.

Then, Carol needs to draw something for her art homework. Alice shows her how to draw nicely.

They then do their English reading homework together.
   "That was a lot of homework!" said Alice.
   "Yes. Now we should play!" said Carol.
The two friends skip into the garden.

1. **What school subject does Carol like?**
   Math ✓

2. **What homework does Alice help Carol with?**
   Art ✓

3. **Who suggests going to play?**
   Carol ✓

4. **Where do the friends go to play?**
   Garden ✓

Andrew's New Pants

Andrew loved his old blue pants.
They were his favorite thing to wear!
His old blue pants felt soft.
His old blue pants had two pockets. Andrew
thought his old blue pants were just right!
One day his mom said that they were going to
the store. She said they were going to buy
some new pants for him.
"Why?" asked Andrew. "
I already have my old blue pants."
"You are getting taller, Andrew," said his mom.
"Your old blue pants are not big enough for you anymore."
Andrew did not like hearing this. He did not want new pants.
At the store, Andrew and his mom looked at all the colors of
pants. There were green pants, black pants, brown pants, gray
pants, and... blue pants! When Andrew tried on the new blue
pants, he realized they felt soft. He realized that they had two
pockets. He realized that they were just right!

1. Where did Andrew and his mom go?
   to the store ☑
2. How many pockets did Andrew's pants have?
   two ☑
3. How did Andrew's pants feel? soft ☑
4. Why did Andrew need new pants?
   a. There were holes in his old pants.
   b. Andrew didn't like the color blue.
   c. Andrew was getting taller. ☑
   d. The old pants had no pockets.

Danielle and the Dinosaurs

Danielle was spending the day with her family in the city.
They were visiting a museum. When they arrived, they got a
map of all the exhibits in the museum.
"What should we look at first?" asked her dad.
"Which way should we go?" asked her mom.
Danielle looked at the map. There were many exhibits, but
Danielle knew where she wanted to go!
"Let's go to see the dinosaurs!" Danielle said excitedly.
"That is where I want to go too!" said Danielle's little sister.
They followed the map to the dinosaur exhibit.
"Wow! Look how big they are!" Danielle said.
She was amazed at the giant dinosaur bones
that were in the exhibit. Danielle liked
the Triceratops dinosaur the best.
Danielle and her family spent most of
their visit looking at the dinosaurs.
It was a wonderful day at the museum!

1. Where was the museum? in the city ☑
2. Which dinosaur was Danielle's favorite?
   a. Stegosaurus
   b. Tyrannosaurus Rex
   c. Brontosaurus
   d. Triceratops ☑
3. What did the family use to help find their way
   to the dinosaur exhibit? a map ☑
4. Does Danielle have a little brother or a little sister?
   little sister ☑

Joey and the Lost Book

Joey loved to read books. He liked books about animals. He
liked books about outer space. He liked books about sports.
Reading books was his favorite activity.
Last week Joey borrowed three books from the library. He was
very careful with these books. He never got them dirty and was
careful not to rip the pages.
"We are going to the library today," said Joey's mom. "Please
gather your three library books to return."
Joey went to gather his books. He kept them in his bedroom. Two
books were on his shelf, but one book was missing! Joey felt
worried. He had never lost a book before...where could it be?
Joey looked under his bed, but it was not there. Joey looked in
the kitchen, but it was not there. Joey looked on the couch in
the family room, but it was not there.
Joey had one more place to look.
He went to his sister's bedroom.
She was reading his book!
"I like to read books too!" said his sister.
Joey felt so happy that he finally found the book!

1. What is Joey's favorite activity?
   reading books ☑
2. How many books did Joey get from the library?
   three ☑
3. In which room of the house is the couch?
   a. The kitchen
   b. The bedroom
   c. The family room ☑
   d. The bathroom
4. Who was reading the lost book? Joey's sister ☑

Molly's Special Day

There was a big calendar hanging on the wall of the kitchen.
Molly looked at it and felt very excited. Only one more day to
wait. Tomorrow was Molly's special day!
Molly's mom was getting ready for the special day by baking a
cake. It was going to be a chocolate cake with chocolate
frosting and strawberries on top.
Molly's dad was getting ready for the special day by working on
a surprise present for Molly.
It was hidden in the garage under a big sheet.
Molly's sisters were getting ready for the special day by hanging
up decorations. They used colorful streamers and balloons to
make the house look so pretty.
"I can't wait for tomorrow!" exclaimed Molly.
"It is going to be my special day!"
Can you guess why tomorrow
is going to be special for Molly?
It is going to be her birthday!

1. In which room of the house was the calendar?
   the kitchen ☑
2. How did Molly's sisters make the house look pretty?
   a. They painted the walls a new color.
   b. They washed the floor.
   c. They hung up decorations. ☑
   d. They planted flowers.
3. What kind of fruit was on the cake? strawberries ☑
4. Where was Dad hiding Molly's present?
   in the garage or under a big sheet ☑

Owen's New Neighbors

The house next door to Owen's house was empty.
Owen felt sad that he did not have any neighbors.
One morning Owen woke up to loud noises.
He didn't know where they were coming from.
Owen looked out his window and saw that
there was a big truck.
People were moving things from
the big truck into the empty house next door.
He saw a man moving a table.
He saw a woman moving a large box.
He saw a boy moving a suitcase.
"Mom! Dad!" Owen shouted. "Look what is happening outside!"
"Yes," said his mom, "we are getting new neighbors!"
"The new neighbors are a family with a mom,
a dad, and a boy the same age as you!" said his dad.
Owen became very excited.
He and his mom baked cookies to bring to the new neighbors.
Owen did not feel sad anymore!

1. Why did Owen feel sad?
   he did not have any neighbors ☑
2. How many people are in the new family next door?
   three_____ ☑
3. What did Owen and his mom bake for his new neighbors?
   cookies_____ ☑
4. What was the boy moving into the house?
   a. A table
   b. A teddy bear
   c. Some fruit
   d. A suitcase ☑

The Big Surprise

The telephone rang at Gavin's house. It was his friend Charlie.
"Can you come to my house?" Charlie asked.
"Yes, I can come in the afternoon," said Gavin.
"Great," said Charlie, "I have a big surprise to show you!"
Gavin wondered what the surprise could be. Was the surprise a
new toy? Was the surprise a new book? Was the surprise a cake?
He was excited to see the surprise!
After Gavin ate his lunch, his mom drove him to Charlie's house.
Charlie was waiting by the door with a big smile.
"Come inside to see the big surprise!" said Charlie.
Gavin walked into the house and saw
Charlie's surprise! The surprise was a new puppy!
The puppy had brown fur and a curly tail.
Gavin thought the puppy was very cute!
"This puppy is a very big surprise!"
said Gavin happily.

1. What was Charlie's surprise?
   a. a new book
   b. a puppy ☑
   c. a cake
   d. a new toy
2. Who drove Gavin to Charlie's house?
   his mom_____ ☑
3. What color was the puppy?
   brown_____ ☑
4. When did Gavin go to Charlie's house,
   in the afternoon or in the morning? in the afternoon ☑

The Night Hike

Tristan was going camping with his dad. They were going
camping in the woods.
During the daytime, Tristan and his dad did many fun activities.
They went fishing, and they swam in the lake. They played some
card games, and they went on a nature hike.
"I like to see trees and animals in the woods. I like to see all of
nature!" Tristan said while they were on the hike.
His dad said, "Did you know there are some
parts of nature we can only see at night?"
Tristan was surprised. He thought that
at night it would be too dark to see anything.
That evening before they went to sleep
in their tent, Tristan's dad said,
"Let's go on a night hike!" On the night hike,
Tristan saw animals that had been sleeping
during the daytime. He saw the moon and
many stars shining in the dark sky.
Tristan loved seeing nature on their night hike!

1. With whom did Tristan go camping?
   his dad_____ ☑
2. What did they do in the lake?
   a. washed the dishes
   b. rode in a boat
   c. went skiing
   d. went fishing and swimming ☑
3. Name three things that Tristan saw on the night hike.
   animals, the moon, stars ☑
4. What kind of games did they play?
   card games_____ ☑

The Orchestra

Adrian was having a good day at school. It was Friday, and on
Fridays his class always went to Mr. Smith's room to learn about
music. Adrian thought that Mr. Smith was a fun music teacher!
"Have you ever heard an orchestra perform?" asked Mr. Smith.
Most of the students in Adrian's class said they had never heard
an orchestra perform. But not Adrian!
"Yes!" said Adrian. "I heard an orchestra perform!
I went to a concert in the city with my family."
Adrian told the class about going to the orchestra concert.
He told them about the violins, the violas, and the basses.
He told them about the trumpets, the tubas,
and the oboes. He told them about his favorite
instrument of all—the cello!
Mr. Smith felt very pleased that Adrian knew
so much about orchestras. Mr. Smith and
the class then listened to some orchestra music.
Adrian really enjoyed it!

1. What day of the week did Adrian's class
   go to Mr. Smith's room? Friday_____ ☑
2. Where did Adrian go to see the orchestra concert?
   In the city_____ ☑
3. What did the class listen to with Mr. Smith?
   orchestra music____ ☑
4. Which orchestra instrument is Adrian's favorite?
   a. the cello ☑
   b. the violin
   c. the tuba
   d. the viola

Name:

The Piano Lesson

Natalie's cousin Patrick knew how to play the piano.
She loved to hear him play.
Natalie dreamed of learning
how to play the piano too!

One day Natalie visited Patrick's house.
She admired his big piano with its
many black and white piano keys.

"Natalie, do you want to play the piano?" asked Patrick.
"Yes, I do!" Natalie exclaimed.
"Let's have a piano lesson!" said Patrick.
Patrick showed Natalie how to place her fingers on the piano keys.
He taught Natalie a simple song. Natalie felt very excited.
"Who is making such beautiful music?" asked her mom when she
walked into the room. "I am!" exclaimed Natalie.
"Patrick gave me a piano lesson!"
"Natalie is a wonderful piano student," said Patrick.
"Thank you, Patrick!" she said and gave her cousin a big hug.

1. What does Natalie dream about?
   learning how to play the piano ☑
2. Who is Natalie's cousin?
   Patrick ☑
3. Where is the piano?
   a. In the school
   b. In Patrick's house ☑
   c. In a store
   d. In Grandma's house
4. How does Natalie feel when playing the piano?
   excited ☑

Name:

The Rainy Day

Mia felt disappointed as she watched the drops of rain slide down
the car window. She and her dad were going to visit her grandma
and grandpa's house.
When Mia visited her grandma and grandpa, she liked to play in
their big yard and look for sunny day treasures there. Mia liked to
find pretty flowers growing in the grass. She liked to look for colorful
rocks near the trees. She could not do these things in the rain.
Mia's grandpa was waiting by the door when they arrived.
"Come Mia! I want to show you something," said her grandpa.
They looked at some old photographs in a big book. The
photographs were of Mia's dad when he was younger. Mia liked
seeing the old photographs.
"Come Mia! I want to show you something," said her grandma.
They looked at a closet filled with old games and puzzles. They
belonged to Mia's dad when he was younger.
Mia liked playing with them.
Mia felt happy. The inside of her grandma and
grandpa's house was filled with rainy day treasures…
photographs, games, puzzles, and, best of all,
her grandma and grandpa!

1. Why was Mia feeling disappointed?
   it was raining or she couldn't play
   in her grandparents' yard/outside ☑
2. What did Mia's grandpa show her? old photographs ☑
3. What was in the closet?
   a. Games and puzzles ☑
   b. Hats and mittens
   c. Cookies and candy
   d. A new computer
4. How did Mia feel at the end of the story? happy ☑

Name:

A Day at the Beach

Caroline woke up early. She felt excited about today. Her family
was going to the beach! Her mom, her dad, her sister, and her
brother were all going to the beach.
At the beach, Caroline liked to play in the sand
with her sister. They used a little shovel and a pail to
help them build a sandcastle. They imagined that
a princess lived in the sandcastle!
Caroline and her brother went swimming in the water. Their dad
went swimming too. The water felt so good after playing in the
hot sun. Caroline had fun jumping in the waves!
"Time for lunch!" called Caroline's mom.
"Hooray!" shouted Caroline. She felt very hungry!
The family ate sandwiches and chips. They also ate some
apples and cookies. The lunch tasted so good!
"A day at the beach is the best kind of day!"
exclaimed Caroline.

1. Which people went swimming?
   Caroline, her brother, and her dad ☑
2. What kind of fruit did they eat? apples ☑
3. What did Caroline and her sister use to build the sandcastle?
   a. a little shovel and a pail ☑
   b. a big bag and a spoon
   c. a comb and a little shovel
   d. a bowl and a big spoon
4. Which meal of the day did the family eat at the beach?
   lunch ☑

Name:

Amy's Vacation

Amy and her family were going on
a big vacation. They were going to
Disney World! Disney World was very far
from Amy's home. They were going to fly to
Disney World by airplane.
Amy was nervous about flying in an airplane. She had never
been in one before. She was not sure if she would like being so
high up in the sky!
On the airplane, Amy was surprised to see so many seats! She
sat in a seat between her mom and her dad.
"Now you need to put on your seatbelt," said her dad. He
showed Amy how to put on the seatbelt.
Amy's mom held her hand. She knew that Amy felt a bit nervous.
The airplane started to move. It went very fast! Soon they were
up in the air!
"Look!" said her mom. Amy looked out the little window. She
could see the world below. It looked so tiny! Amy was not
nervous anymore. She was enjoying the airplane ride!

1. Where was Amy going on vacation? Disney World ☑
2. How did Amy feel before going on the airplane?
   nervous ☑
3. What did Amy's dad show her how to do?
   how to put on the seatbelt ☑
4. What did Amy see out the window?
   a. the airplane
   b. the birds
   c. the world below ☑
   d. her mom

Colors in the Sky

One rainy day Marie was using her crayons to draw a picture.
The picture was a present for her grandma. Marie was drawing
a picture of pink, purple, and yellow flowers.
Marie's grandma was coming to her house to visit. When Marie
was done drawing the picture, she waited for her grandma by
the window. Marie felt happy that her grandma was coming!
"Grandma is here!" Marie exclaimed when she saw Grandma's
big white car.
Marie ran to the door with the picture for her grandma.
"I have a colorful surprise for you, Grandma!" Marie said when
she opened the door for her grandma.
"And I have a colorful surprise for you!"
said her grandma. "Look!"
Marie's grandma pointed to the sky.
There was a beautiful rainbow!
Marie loved seeing all the colors in the sky!

1. What did Marie use to draw the picture?
   crayons ☑
2. How did Marie's grandma get to Marie's house?
   a. by train
   b. by car ☑
   c. by airplane
   d. by bus
3. Where was Marie waiting for her grandma?
   by the window ☑
4. What colorful surprise did Marie's grandma show to Marie?
   a rainbow ☑

Gregory's Trip to the Moon

Gregory looked at the night sky.
He liked to see the moon. He told his mother,
"I will go to the moon." She laughed and told him
it was time to go to sleep.
The next day, Gregory woke up and looked outside.
It was a very windy day. He looked at the sky and could
still see the moon a little bit.
Gregory went downstairs and grabbed his biggest kite. He ran
outside. He flew his kite. The wind pulled the kite very quickly,
and he went up with it!
He looked up and saw that he was moving very close to
the moon! A few minutes later, he landed on the moon
and started to look around.
He was very excited to be on the moon, but he soon became
lonely. Then he remembered something he had learned in school:
there was no wind on the moon! How would he ever get back?
Gregory woke up and realized it was a dream. He laughed. He was
very happy to be on Earth.

1. Who told Gregory to go to sleep?
   his mother ☑
2. Was the weather outside very windy or very snowy?
   very windy ☑
3. What did Gregory use to get to the moon?
   a. a plane
   b. a boat
   c. a kite ☑
   d. a truck
4. Did Gregory really go to the moon?
   No (it was a dream) ☑

Lisa's New School

Lisa felt nervous. Tomorrow was her first day at a new school. Her
family had just moved to a new town, and she did not know any
other children at the new school. She did not know her new teacher.
"Do not worry," said her mother. "You will make a new friend."
"Do not worry," said her father. "Your new teacher will be nice."
The next morning Lisa woke up early. She put on her favorite red
sweater. Her mother walked with her to the new school.
"Hello! My name is Miss Hoover. I am your new teacher!" said a lady
who was standing by the door. She showed Lisa to the classroom.
Lisa walked into the classroom. There were many children there.
One girl smiled at Lisa.
She was wearing a red sweater too!
"Hi! My name is Janine.
Do you want to sit by me?" said the girl.
Lisa smiled. She did not feel nervous anymore.
She had a new friend!
Lisa liked her new school!

1. Why was Lisa going to a new school?
   Her family moved to a new town. ☑
2. What color was Lisa's favorite sweater?
   red ☑
3. Who is Miss Hoover?
   Lisa's new teacher ☑
4. What is the name of Lisa's new friend?
   a. Isabel
   b. Janine ☑
   c. Amy
   d. Lisa

Nate Goes to the Zoo

Nate was so excited when he woke up. Today his family was
going to the zoo! Nate got out of bed. He ate his breakfast.
He brushed his teeth. Now he was ready to go!
"I am ready!" Nate said happily.
"Great! Let's go!" said his mom.
Nate got in the car with his mom and his dad. They drove for a
long time. Finally, they arrived at the zoo.
Nate saw many animals at the zoo.
First, he saw a monkey. The monkey was swinging in a tree.
The monkey was silly! Nate laughed at the monkey.
Next, Nate saw an elephant.
The elephant was very big and very tall.
Nate liked the elephant's big ears.
Last, Nate saw a lion. The lion roared.
The lion's roar was so loud!
Nate liked to roar too!
Nate felt happy to see so many animals.
Nate had so much fun at the zoo!

1. Who went with Nate to the zoo?
   his mom and his dad or his family ☑
2. Which animal was very big and tall?
   the elephant ☑
3. Which animal roared?
   a. a monkey
   b. an elephant
   c. a lion ☑
   d. a horse
4. Did Nate have fun at the zoo?
   yes ☑

Phoebe's Clean Teeth

Every morning and every evening,
Phoebe brushed her teeth.
She had a pink toothbrush.
She had toothpaste that tasted like mint.
Phoebe tried to do a very good job of
brushing her teeth.
One day Phoebe's mom said they were going to the dentist.
"Why do I need to visit the dentist?" asked Phoebe.
"I already keep my teeth very clean."
"The dentist will check your teeth and make sure that they are healthy," Phoebe's mom told her.
Phoebe felt nervous about going to the dentist. Phoebe thought that maybe it would hurt when the dentist checked her teeth.
Phoebe and her mom drove to the dentist's office. The dentist's name was Dr. Stokes. He had a big chair in his office that Phoebe sat in while he checked her teeth.
"Phoebe, you have very clean teeth!" exclaimed Dr. Stokes. "I can see you do a good job brushing them."
Phoebe smiled a great big smile, showing her clean teeth to all!

1. What color was Phoebe's toothbrush?
   a. Blue
   b. Green
   c. Yellow
   d. Pink ☑
2. When did Phoebe brush her teeth?
   every morning and every evening ☑
3. Who was Phoebe's dentist?
   Dr. Stokes ☑
4. How do you think Phoebe felt at the end of the story?
   happy, excited, or relieved ☑

The Fancy Restaurant

Steven and his family were all getting dressed in their best clothes. It was a special day. It was his parents' wedding anniversary!
To celebrate the anniversary, they were going to a restaurant. They were going to a fancy restaurant.
At the restaurant, Steven saw the waiters all wearing tuxedos. The tables of the restaurant had candles and flowers, and fancy tablecloths. Steven wasn't sure if he liked being in such a fancy place.
"I think you will like the food at the restaurant," said his dad.
"I am not sure," said Steven. "It is very fancy, and I never had fancy food before."
"It is good to try new things," said Steven's mom.
When the food arrived, Steven tasted a small bite of it. It was delicious! Steven loved the fancy food!
He ate everything on his plate!
"Happy Anniversary, Mom and Dad!"
said Steven.
"I am glad that we are celebrating
at this fancy restaurant!"

1. Why was Steven's family celebrating?
   a. It was his birthday.
   b. It was the last day of school.
   c. Dad got a new job.
   d. It was his parents' anniversary. ☑
2. Name one thing on the tables at the restaurant.
   candles or flowers or tablecloths ☑
3. What were the waiters wearing?
   tuxedos ☑
4. Did Steven like the fancy food?
   yes (he thought it was delicious) ☑

The Secret Ingredient

Kenneth was spending the weekend at his Aunt Rose's house. He was very excited because this was a special visit. Aunt Rose promised to teach Kenneth how to bake.
Aunt Rose knew how to bake delicious desserts. Her sugar cookies and chocolate brownies always tasted so good! She also made cakes filled with cream and fruit. Kenneth wondered what kind of desserts they would bake together.
"Kenneth, we are going to bake a very special recipe," said Aunt Rose. "We are making a recipe with a secret ingredient!"
"What is it?" asked Kenneth excitedly.
"We are baking my famous banana bread!" said Aunt Rose.
Aunt Rose taught Kenneth how to mash up
the bananas. She taught him how to measure
the sugar and the flour. She helped him
to stir it all up in a big bowl.
"And now for the secret ingredient," said Aunt Rose.
"Love!" Aunt Rose gave Kenneth a big hug!

1. Where was Kenneth spending the weekend?
   at his Aunt Rose's house ☑
2. What was Aunt Rose going to teach to Kenneth?
   how to bake ☑
3. What was the secret ingredient?
   a. candy
   b. love ☑
   c. salt
   d. chocolate
4. In what kind of dish did Kenneth stir up the ingredients?
   a bowl or a big bowl ☑

Tommy Plays Baseball

Every Saturday, Tommy went to the park. He often watched the older kids who played baseball there. Tommy wished that he could play baseball too.
Tommy asked the older kids, "Can I play baseball too?"
"No," said the older kids, "you are too young."
Tommy felt sad. He sat near the baseball field to see them play.
All of a sudden, one of the older kids hit the ball very far. It flew in the air all the way to where Tommy was sitting. Tommy jumped to his feet and caught the ball!
The whole team of older kids cheered for Tommy!
They couldn't believe a younger boy could
make such a great catch!
"You are a great baseball player!"
they said to Tommy.
"Next Saturday, you can join the team!"
"Thanks!" said Tommy proudly.

1. Where did Tommy go on Saturdays?
   to the park ☑
2. What did Tommy wish to do?
   play baseball ☑
3. Why did the older kids not let Tommy play?
   He was too young. ☑
4. How did Tommy show that he could play baseball with them?
   a. He threw the baseball very far.
   b. He played basketball instead.
   c. He caught the baseball. ☑
   d. He stole their baseball.

A Feast for a King!

Ben's Uncle Felix owned a restaurant. Ben loved to go there to watch his uncle cook all the delicious food. He loved the wonderful smells coming from the restaurant's kitchen.

One evening Uncle Felix was coming to Ben's house for dinner.

"Can I help to prepare the food for Uncle Felix?" asked Ben.

"Of course," said his mother. "What should we make?"

"Let's make spaghetti with meatballs, chicken with mushrooms, and steak with potatoes!" said Ben. "Let's also make steamed vegetables with butter sauce and cookies for dessert!"

"Wow!" said his mother, "that is a lot of food!"

"Yes," said Ben, "but Uncle Felix is always cooking a lot for other people, so I want to cook a lot for him!" Ben and his mother spent the whole day preparing all the food.

When Uncle Felix arrived, he saw all the food on the table.

"This is a feast for a king!" exclaimed Uncle Felix.

He gave Ben a hug and sat down to eat the delicious feast!

1. Who owned a restaurant?
   Uncle Felix ☑
2. Which meal of the day was Uncle Felix going to eat at Ben's house?
   dinner ☑
3. What kind of sauce went with the steamed vegetables?
   butter sauce ☑
4. Why did Uncle Felix call the meal a feast for a king?
   a. The king liked spaghetti.
   b. Uncle Felix really was a king.
   c. Ben really was a king.
   d. There was so much food. ☑

Alison's Scary Dream

Alison went to school one day. When she got there, she realized she had forgotten all of her books! The teacher was very angry with her and told her to go home.

When she returned home, she could not find her books anywhere! She looked on the table. She looked under her bed. She decided to look in the closet.

When she opened the closet door, she saw a furry creature hiding in there! It was big and had a long tail. Alison screamed!

Alison's mother ran into Alison's room.

"Wake up, Alison!" said her mother.

"You are having a scary dream!"

Her mother turned the lights on in her bedroom.

Alison opened her eyes. She saw her mother next to her bed. Alison gave her mom a big hug.

Then she told her mom all about the scary dream.

Alison felt much better after talking about it.

She realized that none of the dream was real.

Alison's mom sang her a song to comfort her.

Alison went back to bed and had no more scary dreams!

1. Why was the teacher angry?
   Alison had forgotten all of her books. ☑
2. Name three places Alison looked for her books.
   on the table, under her bed, in the closet ☑
3. What was in Alison's closet?
   a. her books
   b. her puppy
   c. a furry creature ☑
   d. her brother
4. How did Alison's mom comfort her?
   sang her a song ☑

Anthony to the Rescue!

Mrs. Jennifer lived next door to Anthony. She was a nice lady who always let Anthony come over to play with her cat, Mittens. Anthony loved playing with Mittens!

One day Mrs. Jennifer was outside looking all around.

She was very worried.

"What is wrong?" Anthony asked.

"Mittens is lost!" cried Mrs. Jennifer.

"She has been missing for an hour!"

"I will help you find her," said Anthony.

Together they looked by the flowers. Then they looked under the car. They could not find Mittens anywhere!

Suddenly Anthony heard a small sound. He followed the sound to a large apple tree behind Mrs. Jennifer's house.

"Look!" exclaimed Anthony. He pointed to a high tree branch. There was Mittens, stuck high up on the tree.

"I will help!" said Anthony. He carefully climbed into the tree. He rescued Mittens from the high tree branch!

"Thank you, Anthony!" said Mrs. Jennifer. "You saved Mittens!"

1. What kind of pet does Mrs. Jennifer have?
   a. a dog
   b. a fish
   c. a horse
   d. a cat ☑
2. How long had Mittens been missing?
   an hour ☑
3. Where was the large apple tree?
   behind Mrs. Jennifer's house ☑
4. Who saved Mittens?
   Anthony ☑

Cleaning Day

It was a busy day. Alexander and his mom were having their weekly cleaning day! There was much to do on a cleaning day!

"What should we clean first?" asked Alexander.

"Let's begin in your bedroom," said his mom. They dusted all of Alexander's shelves. They washed the sheets from his bed. They put away some of his clothes and books.

"Now, let's clean the family room," said his mom. They vacuumed the rug. They dusted the television. They washed the windows.

"Now, let's clean the kitchen," said his mom. They washed the dirty dishes. They scrubbed the pots and pans. They swept the kitchen floor.

Finally, the whole house was clean.

Alexander felt tired from all the cleaning!

He also felt proud of all the hard work he did with his mom.

"Thank you, Alexander!" said his mom.

"You are such a big help every cleaning day!"

1. Where did they clean first?
   Alexander's bedroom ☑
2. How did they clean the rug in the family room?
   They vacuumed the rug. ☑
3. What did Alexander and his mom scrub?
   pots and pans ☑
4. How did they clean the kitchen floor?
   a. They vacuumed the kitchen floor.
   b. They left the kitchen floor dirty.
   c. They painted the kitchen floor.
   d. They swept the kitchen floor. ☑

Grandpa's Boat

Ellie loved spending time at her grandparents' house. It was near a lake. Her grandpa had a little wooden rowboat on the lake. Her grandpa used two oars to row the boat.

In the summer, Ellie stayed at her grandparents' house. She and her grandpa went on the boat every day. Ellie would wear a life jacket to keep her safe while on the boat. The life jacket would help her float in case she fell into the lake.

They would look for fish in the water. They would wave to the other people who were in other boats. Ellie loved to go on boat rides with her grandpa.

One time Ellie asked if she could row the boat.

"No," said her grandpa, "the oars are too heavy for you. But I have an idea. Let's row together." Ellie sat on her grandpa's lap and together, they used the oars to row the boat. Ellie couldn't wait to tell her grandma that she helped to row grandpa's boat!

1. In which season did Ellie stay at her grandparents' house?
   the summer ☑
2. How did Ellie stay safe while on the boat?
   She wore a life jacket. ☑
3. Who went for boat rides with Ellie?
   her grandpa ☑
4. Why couldn't Ellie row by herself?
   a. The oars were too heavy. ☑
   b. There were too many fish.
   c. There was a hole in the boat.
   d. She lost the oars.

The Chocolate Cake

Today was a special day. It was Robert's dad's birthday. Robert wanted to surprise his dad with a special treat!

"Mom, can you help me bake a special treat for Dad's birthday?" asked Robert.

"Yes," said his mom. "I would like to help you. What kind of treat would you like to bake? Some cookies?"

"I would like to bake a cake!" said Robert. "Dad loves chocolate cake!"

Robert and his mom mixed together flour, sugar, eggs, and lots of chocolate. They put the cake into the oven for 50 minutes. The house smelled so good while the cake was baking!

When the cake was out of the oven, Robert decorated it with colorful candies. Robert thought that the cake looked great! He put the cake on the table.

When Robert's dad came home from work, he was surprised! Robert and his mom put some candles on the cake, and they sang the Happy Birthday song.

Finally, they all ate the delicious chocolate cake!

1. Why was it a special day?
   It was Robert's dad's birthday. ☑
2. What kind of cake did Robert bake?
   Chocolate cake ☑
3. How long did the cake bake in the oven?
   50 minutes ☑
4. Where did Robert put the cake when he was done decorating it?
   a. in the closet
   b. in the oven
   c. on the table ☑
   d. on the floor

The Family Reunion

The big day had finally arrived! The day of the Miller Family Reunion! Olivia, her parents, and her brothers were going to the reunion. She felt very excited!

The family reunion was at a big park. The park was a long distance from Olivia's house. It took two hours to get there!

"We are here!" Olivia's mom said happily when they arrived. Olivia saw the park was decorated with balloons and colorful streamers. There were big tables filled with lots of food.

Many of Olivia's relatives had already arrived, some of the relatives she had never met before. Olivia's mom introduced her to lots of people. There were aunts, uncles, and many cousins. Olivia met one cousin named Jane. Jane was the same age as Olivia. Jane was very nice. Olivia and Jane played many games together. They ate lots of food and had fun the whole day!

The Miller Family Reunion was wonderful. Olivia hoped that they would have another reunion next year!

1. How long did it take to get to the reunion?
   two hours ☑
2. Where was the reunion?
   a. in a forest
   b. at a beach
   c. at Grandma's house
   d. at a park ☑
3. Who introduced Olivia to lots of people?
   her mom ☑
4. Was Jane older than Olivia, younger than Olivia, or the same age as Olivia?
   the same age as Olivia ☑

The Math Test

Stella liked to read. Stella also liked to write. But Stella did not like math. She did not like working on math problems with her class!

On Monday, Stella's teacher said, "On Friday, we will have a math test. Please study Chapter 7 in your math books."

"Oh no!" thought Stella. "I will fail. I do not know how to do the math. I do not understand Chapter 7."

After school, she walked home slowly. She felt worried about the math test. Stella looked very sad when she arrived home.

"What is wrong?" her mom asked.

"My class has a math test on Chapter 7, and I cannot do the math!" Stella said sadly.

"Hmm, maybe these little candies will help! We will use them to help practice doing your math problems!" said her mother.

Stella and her mother practiced all the Chapter 7 math problems using the little candies to help her count out the answers. She never knew that math could be so much fun!

On Friday, Stella took the math test. She got an A+!

"I did it!" said Stella. "Now I do like math!"

1. When is Stella's math test?
   On Friday ☑
2. Does Stella like to write?
   yes ☑

$$a = \sqrt{c^2 - b^2}$$
$$b = \sqrt{c^2 - a^2}$$
$$c = \sqrt{a^2 - b^2}$$

3. How did Stella's mother help?
   a. She told Stella to take a nap.
   b. She practiced with Stella by using little candies. ☑
   c. She sang a song about math.
   d. She ate all of Stella's candies.
4. How did Stella get home from school?
   She walked. ☑

The Perfect Present

There was only one more day until the birthday party
for Hannah's mom. Hannah felt worried because
she still did not have a birthday present for her mom.
"I bought Mom a sweater," said her older sister.
"I bought Mom a necklace," said her older brother.
Hannah did not have much money to buy her mom a big gift.
But she still wanted to give her something special.
"Don't worry, Hannah," said her dad.
"Just give your mom something from your heart."
Hannah thought for a long time and finally decided to give her
something from her heart. She took out her crayons and some
paper. She drew a beautiful picture of her mom.
She wrote, "I love you with all my heart" on the back of the picture.
At the birthday party, Hannah's mom opened her presents.
She liked the sweater and the necklace. She loved the picture!
"This is the perfect present, Hannah!" said her mom.

1. Who bought a sweater for Hannah's mom?
   Hannah's older sister ☑
2. Who bought a necklace for Hannah's mom?
   Hannah's older brother ☑
3. Why couldn't Hannah buy her mom a big gift?
   a. She didn't have much money. ☑
   b. She had too much money.
   c. She didn't like stores.
   d. She didn't like her mom.
4. What did Hannah draw?
   a beautiful picture of her mom ☑

The Snowy Day

Monica lived in the state of Hawaii in the United States.
In Hawaii, Monica could play outside without a coat.
There she could run in the hot sand and splash in the ocean.
In December, the family was going to visit Monica's cousin, Emily.
Emily lived in the state of Indiana. Monica was so excited.
She had never been to Indiana before!
"We will need to pack coats and hats," said Monica's mom.
"Why?" asked Monica. "Will it be cold in Indiana in December?"
"Yes! There may be snow!" said Monica's dad.
Monica could not believe it. She had never seen snow before.
When they arrived in Indiana, there was no snow.
Monica felt disappointed. On the second day in Indiana,
there was still no snow.
On the third day, Emily woke Monica up early.
"Look, Monica!" said Emily. "Look outside!"
Monica looked out the window.
Everything was covered in beautiful white snow!
It sparkled like tiny diamonds all over the ground.
Monica was so happy.
She put on her coat and went outside to play in the beautiful snow!

1. In which state did Monica live?
   Hawaii ☑
2. In which state did Emily live?
   Indiana ☑
3. Monica's family was going to visit Emily in _____.
   a. April   c. July
   b. October   d. December ☑
4. Why did Monica need a coat?
   Monica needed a coat because
   it was cold in Indiana in December. ☑

FUNNY learn PLAY

READING
COMPREHENSION FOR
2ND GRADE

Patrick N. Peerson

Made in United States
Troutdale, OR
09/16/2024

22890005R00055